Take a Stand! World History

Socratic Discussion in History

Teacher Edition

DEDICATION

Dedicated to Zdenka and the De Gree Kids

I. What is The Classical Historian?

The Classical Historian teaches the student to know, understand, engage, and love history. Classical education in history nurtures a young person's natural inclination to seek the truth in all things and trains students to be independent thinkers and lifelong learners. Key in our approach is the Socratic discussion in history.

The Classical Historian provides a comprehensive, classical approach to history effective in classrooms and in the home school. The classical approach challenges students to know history content and to think, read, and write critically about past and current events. Key to this approach is the Socratic discussion in history. The Classical Historian approach is engaging, interesting, and teaches students to be independent thinkers and lifelong learners.

Classical Historian students learn how to analyze history and current events with a critical eye. Students acquire the basic facts of history through a clear concise text and primary source documents. They acquire critical thinking skills specific to history. Using this knowledge and skills, students become adept at finding out the truth in past events. They then use these thinking tools when learning current events.

Students learn how to become a part of the conversation of history by answering key open-ended questions designed to not only test their knowledge of facts but also develop critical thinking skills. Classical Historian students use the Socratic dialog with their classmates or family members and learn to listen to the perspectives of others and grow in their own thinking.

History is not just a list of dates and events but is open to differing interpretations. Classical Historian students know history but also engage the past with critical thinking tools. Students who use these tools in their history class then apply them throughout their lives. We hope you and your student become a part of the conversation.

Grammar, Logic, and Rhetoric

The Classical Historian uses a five-step program to teach history. The first step is the "Grammar of History." Steps two through five are the "Logic and Rhetoric of History." Grammar refers to the basic facts of history; Logic refers to the thinking skills of the historian; Rhetoric refers to the speaking and writing skills of the historian.

1. The Grammar of History
2. The Tools of the Historian
3. Research
4. The Socratic Discussion
5. The Analytical Essay or Reflections

The Grammar of History

The grammar of history refers to the basic facts of an historical event and do not require analytical thinking. Answers to the questions of "who, what, when, and where" constitute the grammar of history. It is essential for a historian to know the grammar of history. Children in the ages of pre-k through grade 5 can handle this stage. Students at this age (3-11) are eager to memorize, parrot, and recite. Even so, learning the grammar of history never stops at a certain age. Even an adult acquires historical knowledge through reading, lectures, visits to museums, and discussions. Because the high school course covers so many years in so short a time, there are not specific words we have chosen for students to remember. Instead, for each chapter the student reads, the student will create a list of 10 important words or terms and write definitions for them.

The Logic and Rhetoric of History
The Dialectic and Rhetoric of History refer to the thinking, speaking, and writing tools essential for analysis and expression in history. They include, as well, the ability to research various sources, engage in Socratic discussions, and write analytical essays.

The Tools of the Historian
The tools of the historian below are taught throughout the Teaching the Socratic Discussion in History curriculum of The Classical Historian. The Classical Historian products show you how to use these tools and train your students how to use them as well.
1. Fact or Opinion?
2. Judgment
3. Supporting Evidence
4. Primary and Secondary Sources
5. Using Quotes
6. Paraphrasing
7. Researching Various Sources
8. The Socratic Discussion in History
9. Making a Counterargument
10. Understanding Cause and Effect
11. Understanding Compare and Contrast
12. Understanding Bias
13. Using Evidence and Not Emotion to Form Judgement
14. Writing a Thesis Statement for an Analytical History Essay
15. Writing an Outline for an Analytical History Essay
16. Writing a Rough Draft for an Analytical History Essay
17. Revising an Analytical History Essay
18. Citing Sources in the Text of an Analytical History Essay
19. Writing a Works Cited Page

Forces that Influence History
In every history, the following forces play in influential role. In our *Take a Stand!* books, we challenge the young historian to analyze the past based on the following forces. For an in-depth explanation of these, please read Carl Gustavson's *A Preface to History*.
1. Technology
2. Social forces
3. Institutional factor
4. Revolution
5. Individual in history
6. The role of ideas
7. Power
8. International organization
9. Causation

10. Loyalty

Research to Answer Open-Ended Questions
Behind every good historian is the research he conducts to form his analysis. The beginning historian, 11 or 12 years old, shouldn't be expected to begin with a long list of resources. Most sixth graders will only need one or two sources to analyze the past. As the child ages, he should use primary source documents, conflicting sources, and as many varied texts that he can. Once the tools of history are learned, the student can use these tools and apply them to various author's interpretations of history, when the time is right.

The active, advanced reader recognizes the bias of the writer, and the active student grasps the importance of primary source documents. There is a problem with a student learning history solely through one perspective. If the child does not learn how to analyze history and practice this analysis on various authors, the student is unprepared to analyze conflicting viewpoints. A well-educated historian should not only be able to form the correct perspective, but also refute a lesser than perfect perspective by using historical analysis.

Because much in history is left up to interpretation, this subject is excellent for the Socratic discussion. Open-ended, interpretive questions are those that are impossible to answer with a simple yes or no, but need explanation. Students learn that it is possible to look at history from varying vantage points. This exercise in logic trains the mind. Questions that will stimulate thought and discussion are such as these:
    1. What caused the Roman Empire from persecuting Christians to adopting Christianity as the state religion?
    2. How did American society change from 1950 to 1990 because of technology?
    3. What caused the fall of the Soviet Union?
    4. Compare and contrast the Incas with the Aztecs.
    5. Compare and contrast the reasons Martin Luther and King Henry VIII founded new religions.

Primary Source Documents
The teacher may assign the students to read primary source documents to help students learn from eyewitness accounts of history. The older the students and the more capable the readers, the more primary source documents can be assigned. We strongly recommend that the first or second time the teacher assigns a primary source document that the teacher reads out loud the document with the students and leads the discussion. With younger students, grades 6-8, the teacher may decide to read the primary source documents together for the entire year. We recommend to assign one primary source document per essay in junior high (grades 6-8) and more for upper grade students.

Questions
The following are question types that historians ask. These questions are found in the *Take a Stand!* books.
    1. Change Over Time
    2. Cause and Effect
    3. Compare and Contrast
    4. Define and Identify

5. Statement/Reaction
6. Evaluation
7. Analyzing Viewpoints

The Socratic Discussion in History

One key element of the tools of learning history for the 12 through 18 year- old is the Socratic discussion. To arrive at the Socratic discussion, students should be able to distinguish between fact and opinion, be able to form good judgment from evidence, and practice analyzing primary and secondary resources. Whereas Socrates used questions to pursue the truth in philosophy, we will use questions to pursue the truth in history.

One point that teachers need never worry about is whether they know enough history to conduct a Socratic discussion. Socrates noted that the best teacher and most intelligent philosopher is one who knows what he does not know. It is essential for the teacher to adopt certain habits of thought and of questioning. Once an interpretive question is chosen and the student has researched and formed a perspective, the teacher needs to ask appropriate questions. Beyond the introductory level of "Who, what, where, and when?" the teacher must ask, "What evidence do you have that supports this?" "Why did this occur?" "How did this occur?" If the evidence is weak, then the student's judgment will be weak as well. For how can there be a strong conclusion with weak evidence? The open discussion stimulates the mind to think of other possible conclusions. The teacher's primary role is to be the one asking the questions and therefore, he doesn't need to be an expert in history.

The teacher's role is not to tell the student what to think, but rather question and challenge the student's conclusions, forcing the student to continually clarify and defend with historical evidence and sound judgment. If other students are available, the teacher can encourage students to debate each other's ideas, with the intention of arriving at the best possible conclusion together. If there are no other students available, the teacher should encourage the student to present a perspective that is contrary to the student's own perspective. In this exercise, the student exercises his mind to view what the opposing side may see. The teacher's goal is to create a scholarly atmosphere where students are free to express their ideas but careful to cite the historical evidence that supports their thesis statement. The Classical Historian DVD and Take a Stand! curriculum teaches the Socratic discussion in history.

Reflections

In this Classical Historian course, teachers may decide to teach and assign one writing assignment per open-ended question. This book has been designed to teach one Reflection Piece per open-ended question. In analytical writing in history, substance takes precedence over style. The student needs to take a perspective that he can defend with evidence and explanation. Writing a narrative which only explains the major points of the Renaissance is not an analytical piece. Writing that Leonardo de Vinci was the most influential artist of the Renaissance and using evidence to defend this point, however, is analytical, because somebody may argue that Michelangelo was more influential.

The *Take a Stand!* series provides questions that compel the student to think and write analytically. Each assignment is crafted so that the student must take a stand on an issue that can be answered from a variety of perspectives. The prewriting activities provided in our Take a Stand! series gives students the necessary guidance to find evidence that will support or refute their thesis.

II. How to Teach with The Classical Historian

This book is designed to make teaching The Classical Historian practical and interesting. You may, as the teacher, start on page 1 and continue to the end of the book, following instructions as you go along. The lessons in this book are designed to be taught once per week with your students for about one hour, and homework suggestions are stated. Of course, the teacher who is teaching more than once per week will have to adjust or modify the program.

Lessons from the book and DVD Curriculum *The Socratic Discussion in History* provide the teacher training in order to teach The Classical Historian. **The teacher needs to begin with this program first.** Watch the DVDs and follow along in the book before you begin teaching students. Understanding how to use these tools correctly prepares teachers to be historians and enables teachers to competently teach and lead Socratic discussions in history and teach analytical writing in history.

Materials Needed
Western Civilization, A Brief History, by Marvin Perry, ISBN 978-1-305-09146-7

Encyclopedia
There are a number of free, online encyclopedias. It is challenging to determine if what is written is true. A good rule to use is that if three our four encyclopedias agree, and if you don't find any disagreement, then most likely, what is written is true.

Take a Stand! World History, Teacher Edition
Take a Stand! World History, Student's Edition

The Socratic Discussion in History DVD Curriculum (only for the Teacher)

Homework
Homework for this course will vary from under one hour to about five hours per week. It depends on how fast the student can read.

Lessons
The lessons designed in this booklet are created for a one or a one-and-a-half-hour class per week.

Ideas to Enrich This History Class That Can Also be Assigned as Homework
Biographies
The best literature to read while studying history is biographies. Biographies are non-fictional and give the students a feeling for the people involved in the history. Once students learn the Socratic discussion approach, it is a great idea to have students deepen their historical studies with biographies.

The Word Game
The Word Game is a simple vocabulary review game. A student chooses one word from the Grammar and describes it without stating the word. The first student to guess the word correctly

"wins." Then, this student chooses the next word to describe. Simple and yet educational, the Word Game is a great way to learn and review important words and terms.

Semester Final:
Sometime before the end of 16 weeks announce to the students that they will be responsible to present to the whole class, and to their parents, two of their essays from the first semester. No note cards are to be used Students do much better in short presentations when they are not reading from notes. One week or two weeks before the presentation, have students do a trial run and present to the class. After each student presents, ask each listening student to say one thing that the presenter did well, and one thing he could improve on. Pay attention to how much time lapsed during the presentation to make sure the student is relaying enough information. For the first semester, a 2-5-minute presentation is fine. Also, in the presentation, the student should not only speak about his perspective, but he can also speak about an opposing perspective, and add the reason why he does not agree with this. The goals of the presentation are:
1. Practice public speaking.
2. Share with the parents and students the knowledge the student has obtained.
3. Advertise to the parents what your students are learning.
4. Highlight and honor students publicly for their work.

All should get dressed up for the presentation. It may be the first time the male student has to wear a tie. And, they will be introduced to the need to look good while making a presentation.

Year Final: I strongly recommend that in the spring, the students, in addition to completing regular class assignments, choose one topic from semester 2 to be an "expert." The student should read a biography from this time period and should also be compelled to research from at least three primary sources not found in the textbook. The student should also know they are responsible for about a 5-10 minute final presentation (or two five minute presentations). Much like the semester final, this final looks the same, however, the student will only present one topic in depth.

A Note on the Presentations
When you announce the requirements for the presentations, realize that at first, the assignment may scare your students. This is normal. Once they present at the semester final, they will see they can do it and it will boost their confidence. Also, because some students excel, or are more academically developed than others, be very gentle during the actual presentation. If the student stumbles, the teacher or the students may ask questions to help the presenter speak. And, do not focus on the number of minutes initially. Basically, whatever the student gives you, acknowledge their work.

Teacher Instructions for Week One: The Earliest Civilizations
During Class
1. Icebreaker: Two Truths and a Lie
   This is an ice breaker I like to use with pre-teens and teenagers. Each person (including the teacher) writes down two truths and a lie about himself, in any order. Then, each person reads out loud the three statements, and everyone guesses which statement is the lie. No matter how well or how poorly the students know each other, an ice breaker activity is recommended. Learning is fun and social, and the ice breaker loosens everyone up. It is FANTASTIC for the students to see a sincere smile from each other and from the teacher before learning happens.

2. Teach the lesson Fact or Opinion in *Take a Stand!*
3. Teach the lesson Judgment in *Take a Stand!*
4. On page 4 of *Western Civilization*, read the Focus Questions. Have students give their best answers out loud.
5. On page 21 of *Western Civilization*, read out loud the Primary Source. Have students discuss answers to the questions on page 21.
6. Introduce students to the open-ended question.
7. If time permits, read one or more primary sources on Mesopotamia, Egypt, and Kush on this website: https://www.classicalhistorian.com/free-primary-sources.html#/. Have students answer the questions in class.
8. Assign students to read chapter 1.

Homework

1. Read chapter 1.
2. Answer the Focus Questions for chapter 1, found on page 4.
3. Complete all activities of the open-ended questions for this chapter except the Reflection.

Teacher Instructions for Week Two: The Ancient Hebrews

During Class

1. Review the Focus Questions from chapter 1 of *Western Civilization*.
2. Review the answers from the Socratic discussion and lead the Socratic discussion from Lesson One. Direct students to write the Reflection.
3. Teach Primary or Secondary Source Analysis and Judgement.
4. On page 23, preview the Focus Questions.
5. Read the primary source on page 32. Direct students to answer the questions out loud.
6. Introduce students to the open-ended question.
7. If time permits, read one or more primary sources on the Ancient Hebrews on this website: https://www.classicalhistorian.com/free-primary-sources.html#/. Have students answer the questions in class.

Homework

1. Read chapter 2 of Western Civilization.
2. Answer the Focus Questions for chapter 2 on page 23.
3. Complete all activities for the two open-ended questions except the Reflection.

Teacher Instructions for Week Three: Ancient Greece

During Class

1. Review the Focus Questions from chapter 2 of *Western Civilization*.
2. Review the answers from the Socratic discussion questions and lead the Socratic discussions. Direct students to write the Reflection on one of the discussions.
3. Teach the lesson on Paraphrasing.
4. On page 34, preview the Focus Questions for chapter 3, The Greeks.
5. Read the primary source on page 61. Direct students to answer the questions out loud.
6. Introduce students to the open-ended question.
7. If time permits, read one or more primary sources on Ancient Greece on this website: https://www.classicalhistorian.com/free-primary-sources.html#/. Have students answer the questions in class.

Homework

1. Read chapter 3 of Western Civilization through page 61.
2. Answer the Focus Questions on pages 34 and 35.
3. Complete the open-ended question.

Teacher Instructions for Week Four: The Hellenistic Age

During Class

1. Review the Focus Questions from chapter 3 of *Western Civilization.*
2. Review the answers from the Socratic discussion question and lead the Socratic discussion. Direct students to write the Reflection on the discussions.
3. Have students share their Reflection in class.
4. Begin reading in class from chapter 3, pages 62-71.

Homework

1. Read pages 62-71 in Western Civilization. Answer the Questions.
2. Answer the open-ended question.

Teacher Instructions for Week Five: Roman Republic and Empire

During Class

1. Review the answers from the Questions on Alexander the Great.
2. Lead the class in the Socratic discussion.
3. Direct the students to write the Reflection for the Socratic discussion.
4. Introduce students to the open-ended discussion on the Roman Republic.
5. If time permits, preview the Focus Question for chapter four on page 72.
6. If time permits, read one or more primary sources on the Roman Republic and Roman Empire on this website: https://www.classicalhistorian.com/free-primary-sources.html#/. Have students answer the questions in class.

Homework

1. Read chapter 4.
2. Answer the Focus Questions on page 72.
3. Answer the open-ended questions.

Teacher Instructions for Week Six: Christianity

During Class

1. Review the answers from the Focus on Questions on page 72.
2. Lead the class in the Socratic discussions.
3. Direct the students to write the Reflection for the Socratic discussion.
4. Introduce students to the open-ended discussion on Christianity.
5. Read out loud the primary source on page 115 and have students answer the question. Review their answers.

Homework

1. Complete the Socratic discussion open-ended assignment.
2. Assign one or more of the primary source readings on Christianity from this website: https://www.classicalhistorian.com/free-primary-sources.html#/. Have students write their answers.

Teacher Instructions for Week Seven: Ancient India

During Class

1. Lead students in the Socratic discussion on Christianity.
2. Direct students to write their Reflection.
3. Introduce students to the Socratic discussion questions on Ancient India. Let students know they are responsible for their own research for these two discussions.

4. Time permitting, read the primary sources on Ancient India and Buddhism and Hinduism on this website: https://www.classicalhistorian.com/free-primary-sources.html#/. Have students write their answers.

Homework

Complete the Socratic discussion open-ended assignments. Students will have to use their own sources to research this topic.

Teacher Instructions for Week Eight: Ancient China

During Class
1. Lead the class in the Socratic discussions on Ancient India.
2. Direct students to write their reflection.
3. Introduce students to the Socratic discussions on Ancient China.
4. Time permitting, read the primary sources on Ancient China on this website: https://www.classicalhistorian.com/free-primary-sources.html#/. Have students write their answers.

Homework

Complete the Socratic discussions on Ancient China. Students will have to use their own sources to research this topic.

Teacher Instructions for Week Nine: The Middle Ages in Europe

During Class
1. Lead the class in the Socratic discussions on Ancient China.
2. Direct students to write their reflection.
3. Introduce students to the Socratic discussion open-ended question for this week.
4. Read out loud the primary source on page 137 and answer the questions in class.
5. Time permitting, read the primary sources on Medieval Europe on this website: https://www.classicalhistorian.com/free-primary-sources.html#/. Have students write their answers.

Homework
1. Read chapter 6 of Western Civilization.
2. Answer the Focus Questions for Chapter 6, found on pages 124 and 125.
3. Complete the Socratic discussion question.

Teacher Instructions for Week Ten: The End of Medieval Civilizations

During Class
1. Review the Focus Questions for Chapter 6.
2. Lead the Socratic discussion from week nine. Direct students to write the reflection.
3. Preview the Focus Questions for chapter 7, found on pages 154-155.
4. Read the primary source found on page 161 out loud. Answer the questions.
5. Introduce students to the open-ended discussions.

Homework
1. Read chapter 7 of *Western Civilization*
2. Answer the Focus Questions for chapter 7.
3. Complete the Socratic discussion open-ended questions.

Teacher Instructions for Week Eleven: Islamic Civilizations

During Class
1. Review the answers for the Focus Questions for chapter 7.
2. Lead the Socratic discussions.
3. Direct students to write their reflection.

4. Introduce students to the Socratic discussions.
5. If time permits, read the primary sources for the Islamic Civilizations out loud in class and have students answer the questions. The primary sources for Islamic Civilizations are located here: https://www.classicalhistorian.com/free-primary-sources.html#/

Homework

Complete all work for the Socratic discussions. Students will have to use their own sources to research this topic.

Teacher Instructions for Week Twelve
Medieval China and Medieval Japan

During Class

1. Lead the class in the Socratic discussions.
2. Direct students to write the reflection.
3. Introduce students to the Socratic discussions for Medieval China and Medieval Japan.
4. If time permits, read the primary sources for Medieval China and Medieval Japan out loud in class and have students answer the questions. The primary sources for Medieval China and Medieval Japan are located here: https://www.classicalhistorian.com/free-primary-sources.html#/

Homework

Complete all activities for the Socratic discussions. Students will have to use their own sources to research this topic.

Teacher Instructions for Week Thirteen: Medieval Africa

During Class

1. Lead the class in the Socratic discussions.
2. Introduce students to the Socratic discussion on Medieval Africa.
3. Read the primary sources for Medieval Africa out loud in class and have students answer the questions. The primary sources for Medieval Africa are located here: https://www.classicalhistorian.com/free-primary-sources.html#/

Homework

Complete the Socratic discussion for Medieval Africa. Students will have to use their own sources to research this topic.

Teacher Instructions for Week Fourteen: The Renaissance

During Class

1. Lead the class in the Socratic discussion.
2. Direct students to write their reflection.
3. Read out loud on page 185 of *Western Civilization*. Have students answer the question in class.
4. Review the Focus Questions 1-5 on page 180 of *Western Civilization.*
5. Read the primary sources for the Renaissance out loud in class and have students answer the questions. The primary sources for Renaissance are located here: https://www.classicalhistorian.com/free-primary-sources.html#/
6. Introduce students to the open-ended question.

Homework

1. Answer Focus Questions 1-5 on page 180 of *Western Civilization*. Read chapter 8.
2. Complete the Renaissance Socratic discussion assignment.

Teacher Instructions for Week Fifteen: The Reformation

During Class

1. Review answers from Focus Questions 1-5 on page 180 of *Western Civilization*.
2. Lead the class in the Socratic discussion for the Renaissance.
3. Introduce students to the Socratic discussion for the Reformation.
4. Read the primary sources for the Reformation out loud in class and have students answer the questions. The primary sources for Reformation are located here: https://www.classicalhistorian.com/free-primary-sources.html#/

Homework
1. Answer Focus Question 6-7 on page 180 of *Western Civilization*. Read chapter 8.
2. Complete the Socratic discussion questions.

Teacher Instructions for Week Sixteen
Absolutism, The Age of Exploration, The Commercial Revolution

During Class
1. Review the answers to Focus Questions 6-7 on page 180 of Western Civilization.
2. Lead the class in the Socratic discussion.
3. Direct students to write the Reflection.
4. Read the primary sources for the Reformation and the Age of Exploration out loud in class and have students answer the questions. The primary sources are located here: https://www.classicalhistorian.com/free-primary-sources.html#/
5. Introduce students to the open-ended question.

Homework
1. Read chapter 9 of *Western Civilization*.
2. Answer the Focus Questions on page 204.
3. Complete the Socratic discussion questions.

Teacher Instructions for Week Seventeen
The Scientific Revolution and the Age of Enlightenment

During Class
1. Review answers from Chapter 9 Focus Questions.
2. Lead the class in the Socratic discussion.
3. Direct students to write the Reflection.
4. Read out loud the primary source document on page 240. Answer the question.
5. Introduce students to the open-ended question.

Homework
1. Read chapter 10. Answer the Focus Questions for chapter 10.
2. Complete the open-ended question.

Teacher Instructions for Week Eighteen: The French Revolution

During Class
1. Review the Focus Questions for chapter 10.
2. Lead the Socratic discussion form week seventeen.
3. Read the primary source on page 274 and answer the question.
4. Introduce students to the open-ended question.

Homework
1. Read chapter 11. Answer the Focus Questions for chapter 11.
2. Complete the open-ended questions.

Teacher Instructions for Week Nineteen: The Industrial Revolution

During Class
1. Review the answers for chapter 11.

2. Lead the Socratic discussions.
3. Direct students to write the Reflection.
4. Read the primary source on page 290 of *Western Civilization* and answer the question.
5. Preview the Focus Questions for chapter 12.

Homework
1. Read chapter 12. Answer the Focus Questions for chapter 12.
2. Complete the open-ended question.

Teacher Instructions for Week Twenty: Thought and Culture

During Class
1. Review the answers for chapter 12.
2. Lead the Socratic discussions.
3. Read the primary source document on page 307 and answer the question.
4. Introduce the students to the Open-Ended Questions.

Homework
1. Read chapter 13.
2. Answer the Focus Questions for chapter 13.
3. Prepare for Socratic discussions by answering the open-ended questions.

Teacher Instructions for Week Twenty-One: Liberalism and Nationalism

During Class
1. Review the answers to the Focus Questions for chapter 13.
2. Review all the answers from the questions in the Take a Stand! book.
3. Read the primary source on page 321 and answer the question.
4. Preview the Focus Questions for chapter 14 of Western Civilization.
5. Preview with students the open-ended question.

Homework
1. Read chapter 14 of Western Civilization.
2. Answer the Focus Questions for chapter 14.
3. Answer the open-ended questions for chapter 14.

Teacher Instructions for Week Twenty-Two
Thought and Culture in the 19th Century

During Class
1. Review the answers to the Focus Questions for chapter 14.
2. Lead the class in the Socratic discussions from Week Twenty-One.
3. Direct students to write the Reflection. Have students share what they wrote.
4. Read the primary source and answer the question on page 338.
5. Preview the Socratic discussions.

Homework
1. Read chapter 15.
2. Answer the Focus Questions for chapter 15.
3. Answer the Socratic discussions.

Teacher Instructions for Week Twenty-Three: The Age of Imperialism

During Class
1. Review the Focus Questions for chapter 15.
2. Lead the Socratic discussions. Direct students to write their reflection.
3. Read the primary source on page 365 and answer the question.
4. Introduce students to the open-ended question.

Homework
1. Read chapter 16.
2. Answer the Focus Questions for chapter 16.
3. Answer the open-ended question.

Teacher Instructions for Week Twenty-Four: Modern Consciousness

During Class
1. Review the Focus Questions from chapter 16.
2. Lead the Socratic discussion.
3. Direct students to write the Reflection.
4. Introduce students to the Focus Questions for chapter 17.
5. Read out loud the primary source on page 385 and answer the question.
6. Introduce students to the Socratic discussion questions.

Homework
1. Read chapter 17.
2. Answer the Focus Questions for chapter 17.
3. Prepare for the Socratic discussions

Teacher Instructions for Week Twenty-Five
Causes and Effects of World War I

During Class
1. Review the answers to the Focus Questions for chapter 17.
2. Lead the class in the Socratic discussions.
3. Direct students to write the reflection.
4. Preview the Focus Questions for chapter 18.
5. Read the primary source on page 406.
6. Introduce students to the Socratic discussion

Homework
1. Read chapter 18.
2. Answer the Focus Questions for chapter 18.
3. Complete the Socratic discussions.

Teacher Instructions for Week Twenty-Six: Totalitarianism

During Class
1. Review the Focus Questions for chapter 18.
2. Lead the class in the Socratic discussions.
3. Direct students to write their reflection.
4. Introduce students to chapter 19 and preview the Focus Questions.
5. Read the primary source on page 458 and answer the question.
6. Research the Communist Manifesto and show students where on the internet this is available.

Homework
1. Read chapter 18.
2. Read the Communist Manifesto.
3. Answer the Focus Questions for chapter 19.
4. Complete the Socratic discussion work.

Teacher Instructions for Week Twenty-Seven: Causes of World War II

During Class
1. Review the Focus Questions for chapter 19.
2. Lead the class in the Socratic discussion.

3. Direct students to write the reflection.
4. Introduce students to Chapter 20 and the Socratic discussion.

Homework
1. Read pages 475-479 in Western Civilization.
2. Complete the Socratic discussion.

Teacher Instructions for Week Twenty-Eight: World War II

During Class
1. Lead the students in the Socratic discussion.
2. Direct students to write the reflection.
3. Read the primary source on page 492 and answer the question.
4. Preview the Focus Questions on page 475.
5. Introduce students to the Socratic discussion questions.

Homework
1. Read chapter 20.
2. Answer all of the Focus Questions for chapter 20.
3. Complete the Socratic discussion questions.

Teacher Instructions for Week Twenty-Nine
The Beginning of the Cold War

During Class
1. Review the answers to the Focus Questions for chapter 20.
2. Lead the class in the Socratic Discussions
3. Direct students to write the reflection.
4. Read the primary source on page 502 and write the reflection.
5. Research Winston Churchill's "Iron Curtain Speech." Show it during class or read it together in class.

Homework
1. Read chapter 21.
2. Answer the Focus Questions for chapter 21.
3. Research what was decided at the Yalta Agreement.
4. Complete the Socratic discussions.

Teacher Instructions for Week Thirty: The End of the Cold War

During Class
1. Review the answers to the Focus Questions for chapter 21.
2. Lead the class in the Socratic discussions.
3. Introduce the students to the Socratic Discussion.

Homework
1. Complete the answers for the Socratic discussions.
2. Research information outside of the Western Civilization to learn about the roles of President Reagan and Pope John Paul II to learn about the roles these two played in ending the Cold War.

Teacher Instructions for Week Thirty-One
The Post-Cold War World and Islamic Terrorism

During Class
1. Lead the class in the Socratic discussion.
2. Direct students to write the reflection.
3. Introduce students to the Focus Questions for chapter 22.

Homework
1. Read chapter 22.
2. Answer the Focus Questions for chapter 22.
3. Answer the Socratic discussion open-ended questions.

Teacher Instructions for Week Thirty-Two: Final Class

During Class
1. Review answers for the Focus Questions for chapter 22.
2. Lead the class in the Socratic discussions.
3. Direct students to write the reflection.
4. Have a discussion about which topic was the favorite topic of students to study this year.

Week One: The Earliest Civilizations

Fact or Opinion?
Fact

A **fact** in history is a statement that is accepted as true and is not debatable. A fact often refers to a date, a person, or a document. For example, "The Declaration of Independence was written and signed in 1776." We know this happened because we have the original document, the men who wrote and signed this document wrote about it, and observers wrote about it as well. There is no doubt in anybody's mind whether the facts in this statement are true.

Which of these sentences are facts and which are not?

Fact or Not a Fact?		
NF	1.	The first Egyptian settlements were near the Euphrates River.
F	2.	Early civilizations often settled near major rivers.
F	3.	Another way of saying Old Stone Age is Paleolithic.
NF	4.	Early man used guns to hunt buffaloes.
NF	5.	California has the best waves to surf in the United States.

Opinion

An **opinion** is an expression of somebody's ideas and is debatable. Opinions that are based on facts and good reasoning are stronger than opinions not based on facts. In history, opinions alone tend to be less persuasive than when a person supports his opinions with facts.

Are the following opinions or facts?

Opinion or Fact?		
O	1.	Life for early man was more peaceful than our life today.
O	2.	Teachers who are nice don't assign homework.
O	3.	Almost everybody's favorite food is pizza.
F	4.	Mesopotamia means "the land between two rivers."
F	5.	Sumerians were the first people to use wheeled vehicles.

Now that you've learned the difference between fact and opinion, read the example paragraphs below and answer the questions. These two students attempted to answer the question "Did the ancient civilizations of Mesopotamia contribute much to world civilizations?"

Student 1: The ancient civilizations of Mesopotamia contributed much to the world. These societies rocked! When there was a really big war, the Sumerians and Assyrians knew how to fight hard. These societies would use a lot of arrows in their battles, and the enemy wouldn't know how to respond. Most of the time, the enemy would just die, or quit. Also, everyone knows that Mesopotamia had the best kind of clothing. Have you seen pictures of the great Babylonian kings? Their clothing was "tight." And, Mesopotamia was the land between two rivers, so therefore this area had to have a lot of water. All in all, the ancient civilizations of Mesopotamia contributed much to the world.

Student 2: The ancient civilizations of Mesopotamia contributed much to the world. The Sumerians created the first written language. We call this "Cuneiform." Sumerians also were the first people to use the wheel for transportation. The Babylonian king Hammurabi established one of the first written law codes, known as Hammurabi's Code. These laws helped the weak against the strong, protected women's property rights, and regulated doctors' fees. Also, the Hittites discovered how to use iron, which at that time was the strongest metal in the world that humans could work with. Phoenicians gave us the world's first alphabet, with 22 symbols. In addition, the Hebrews were the first people ever to worship only one God. Yes, the ancient civilizations of Mesopotamia contributed much to the world.

Questions

1. Which of these two students uses more opinion than fact? <u>Student 1 uses more opinion than fact.</u>

2. Copy one sentence that is an opinion. <u>Also, everyone knows that Mesopotamia had the best kind of clothing.</u>

3. Copy one sentence that details at least one fact. <u>The Babylonian king Hammurabi established one of the first written law codes, known as Hammurabi's Code.</u>

4. Which of these two students' writings is more persuasive? Why? <u>Student 2 has a more persuasive essay than Student 1 because student 2 uses more facts than opinions for the supporting evidence.</u>

Judgment

Judgment in social studies means a person's evaluation of facts. For example, if we use the fact that the Romans believed citizens could vote, we can judge from this that the Romans looked somewhat favorably on democracy. Good judgment is very persuasive but bad judgment is not.

Write facts and judgments in the spaces provided. Discuss your judgments in class.

Fact: 11-year-old Maria Perez won the gold medal in the city 800-meter sprint.	
Judgment: Maria is a fast runner.	
Fact: Private Smith was killed in war and had one wife and 7 children.	
Judgment: Private Smith's death was a tragedy.	
Fact: Thursday's temperature in Santa Ana was 105 degrees Fahrenheit.	
Judgment: Thursday was very hot.	

Make your own.

Fact:
Judgment:

Fact:
Judgment:

Fact:
Judgment:

Socratic Discussion Open-Ended History Question
Mesopotamia, Egypt, and Kush

Many of the world's earliest civilizations were located in Mesopotamia and Egypt. The great rivers of the Nile, the Euphrates, and the Tigris were centers of these societies, which have given mankind great contributions. Spanning from about the year 4000 B.C. to 350 A.D., incredible inventions, discoveries, and new ways of thought emerged from these lands.

Answer the question "What are the two most important contributions to the world made by the ancient civilizations of Mesopotamia, Egypt, and Kush?" Explain which civilization is responsible for the contributions you choose, and explain how these contributions are important to us today.

Ancient Civilizations of Mesopotamia, Egypt, and Kush

Research the greatest contributions of civilizations of Mesopotamia, Egypt, and Kush. Write fifteen contributions, which civilization was responsible for them, and what this contribution means to world civilizations today. Below are listed the major ancient civilizations of Mesopotamia, Egypt, and Kush.

Sumeria (c. 4000–2300 B.C.)
Hittite (c. 1600–1200 B.C.)
Hebrew (c. 1200–600 B.C.)
Chaldea (c. 605–539 B.C.)
Ancient Egypt (c. 3000–343 B.C.)

Babylonia (c. 2300–1600 B.C.)
Phoenicia (c. 1200–146 B.C.)
Assyria (c. 1100–650 B.C.)
Persia (c. 550–330 B.C.)
Kush (c. 1070 B.C.–A.D. 350)

CONTRIBUTIONS

Contributions	Civilization
1. The wheel	1. Sumeria
2. Cuneiform – a system of writing	2. Sumeria
3. Arch	3. Sumeria
4. Hammurabi's Code	4. Babylonia
5. Lunar Calendar	5. Babylonia
6. 24-hour day, 60-minute hour	6. Babylonia
7. Use of iron	7. Hittite
8. Alphabet with 22 symbols	8. Phoenicia
9. The Old Testament	9. Hebrew
10. Monotheism	10. Hebrew
11. The Ten Commandments	11. Ancient Hebrew
12. Zoroastrianism	12. Persia
13. Hieroglyphs – a system of writing	13. Ancient Egypt
14. Paper	14. Ancient Egypt
15. Geometry	15. Ancient Egypt

Rating the Contributions

Rate the contributions of the various civilizations of Mesopotamia, Egypt, and Kush. Which contribution do you think is the most important? Which is the second most important? Write the origin of the contribution. From which civilization did it come?

Contributions in order of importance	Civilization
1.	1.
2.	2.
3.	3.
4.	4.
5.	5.
6.	6.
7.	7.
8.	8.
9.	9.
10.	10.
11.	11.
12.	12.
13.	13.
14.	14.
15.	15.

Question
What made you decide which were the top three contributions made to world civilizations?_____
_____
_____
_____

Socratic Discussion and Reflection

When you share ideas with other students, your ideas may be reinforced, rejected, or slightly changed. Listening to your classmates' ideas will help you form your own judgment. After the class discussion, write down your answer to the question, "What are the two most important contributions to the world made by the ancient civilizations of Mesopotamia, Egypt, and Kush?" Explain which civilization is responsible for the contributions you choose, and explain how these contributions are important to us today.

_____
_____
_____
_____
_____
_____
_____
_____
_____
_____
_____
_____
_____
_____
_____
_____
_____
_____
_____
_____
_____
_____
_____
_____
_____
_____

Week Two: The Ancient Hebrews
Primary or Secondary Source Analysis

A **primary source** is a piece of evidence authored by a person who witnessed or experienced a historical event. For example, diaries and journals are primary sources. It is usually better to find out something from a person who experienced a particular event than to hear about it secondhand. Primary source documents are usually the most useful for historians.

A **secondary source** is a piece of evidence that has been worked on by somebody who was not a witness to the historical event. Examples of secondary sources are textbooks, documentaries, and encyclopedias. Secondary sources are valuable but not as valuable as primary sources. Secondary sources contain the bias of the writer. This means that the writer of a secondary source will put his ideas into his explanation of the historical event, even when he may be trying not to.

      Take a look at these two examples regarding the same event.
Event: Car accident outside of school

Example 1: "Oh no! I was in the back seat of my mom's car. This kid threw his friend's handball onto the street. All of a sudden, his friend jumped in front of my mom's car to get his ball. He didn't even look if a car was coming. My mom hit him and his body smashed against our windshield. Blood was everywhere!"

Example 2: "Did you hear what happened? Mario told me that his brother was walking home when he dropped his handball onto the street. After his brother looked both ways for cars, he stepped out onto the street to get his ball. Then this mad lady came speeding down the street and aimed her car at him. She hit him on purpose!"

Questions
1. Which is a primary source? Example 1 is a primary source.
2. Which is a secondary source? Example 2 is a secondary source.
3. What is usually more believable, a primary or secondary source? Why? <u>A primary source is usually more believable because the witness saw it firsthand. It's easier to trust somebody who was at the event than somebody who only heard about it.</u>

Using Quotes

A **quote** is when a writer uses the exact words of another writer. An effective analytical essay in social studies will use quotes. For example, an essay about the use of violence in the Middle Ages will be stronger if certain quotes from this time period are used. When you argue a point about the past, there is no better evidence than a primary source document or quote.

Look at the example below. The paragraph is part of an answer to the question "Was the plague a problem in ancient Greece?"

The plague was most certainly a problem to the ancient Greeks. The Greek historian Thucydides, in "The Peloponnesian Wars," wrote, "Words indeed fail one when one tries to give a general picture of this disease; and as for the sufferings of individuals, they seemed almost beyond the capacity of human nature to endure." To the ancient Greeks, the plague was a serious problem.

When using quotes, write the original author's name and the speech or document from which the quote was taken from. Punctuate correctly with quotation marks.

Practice

Practice writing three quotations taken from your textbook. Use correct punctuation! Pay attention to the commas, the quotation marks, and the end marks. For example, Julius Caesar, when crossing the Rubicon River, said, "The die is cast."

1. _____
   _____

2. _____
   _____

3. _____
   _____

Socratic Discussion Open-Ended Question
Ancient Hebrews

In the middle of a large number of civilizations that practiced similar religious beliefs, one group of people emerged which, in many ways, was completely different than its neighbors. The ancient Hebrews, when compared to neighbors such as the Egyptians, the Phoenicians, and the Assyrians, stood out as a distinct group when it came to issues of ethical teachings (what is right and wrong) and central beliefs (religion).

Although the ancient Hebrews were in the minority, many of their beliefs and ideas are reflected in Western civilization today. In many ways, beliefs and ideas of the ancient Hebrews are very similar to beliefs and ideas of modern Americans. Answer the question, "What are two most important contributions the ancient Hebrews of the Old Testament gave to Western civilization?"

What is Western Civilization?

When historians use the term "Western civilization," they are normally talking about societies that share certain ideas and practices together. Many of these ideas and practices came from ancient peoples like the Hebrews, the Greeks, and the Romans. Some of these ideas are a belief in one God (historians call this monotheism), democracy, a society governed by laws, political equality, justice, freedom, and respect for written language.

In this prewriting activity, your goal is to find the continents of the world that are typically associated with being part of Western civilization. By using your textbook, your teacher, your classmates' knowledge, and asking any adult you think may know the answer, complete the following activities. The Hebrews were the first to practice monotheism. The Greeks were the first to practice democracy.

Belief in One God
List the continents where most of the people believe in one God.
1. North America
2. South America
3. Europe
4. Australia
5. Africa

Democracy
List the continents where citizens vote for their leaders.
1. North America
2. South America
3. Europe
4. Australia

Look on a map. The continents that you have listed in both categories are typically known as Western civilization.

Ancient Hebrew Beliefs

Ancient Hebrew beliefs and ideas have had a profound effect on Western civilization. In this activity, read these written laws from the Hebrews, known as the Ten Commandments. Rewrite them, using your own words, and choose two you think are the most important.

The Ten Commandments

1. You should have no other Gods but Me.

2. You shall not make for yourself any idol, nor bow down to it or worship it.

3. You shall not misuse the name of the Lord your God

4. Remember to keep holy the Sabbath day.

5. Honor thy father and mother.

6. You shalt not kill.

7. You shalt not commit adultery.

8. You shalt not steal.

9. You shalt not bear false witness against thy neighbor.

10. You shalt not covet thy neighbor's wife or your neighbor's goods.

Write these in your own words.
1.
2.
3.
4.
5.
6.
7.
8.
9.
10.

QUESTION: Which two do you think are the most important? Why?_____
_____
_____

Contributions of Ancient Hebrews

Using your textbook, write down five contributions the ancient Hebrews have made to Western civilization.

Contributions
1. Monotheism
2. The Old Testament
3. Belief in morality – the idea that there is a right and wrong
4. Christianity – Jesus Christ was Jewish
5. A tradition and respect for written laws

Prioritize
List these five in order of importance.
1.
2.
3.
4.
5.

Question: Why did you list the top two as being most important? _____

_____

_____

Socratic Discussion Open-Ended History Question
People of the Old Testament

The history of Judaism in the Old Testament is rich in historical and heroic figures. Abraham, Moses, Naomi, Ruth, David, and Yochann ben Zaccai have done much to build and preserve the Jewish faith. Considering that this religion has lasted approximately 4000 years and has affected multiple nations of various continents, these people could possibly be some of the most important in all of world history.

Historians will often look at people of history and try to compare them with each other trying to find out who has played the largest role in preserving the faith. Defend or reject the statement "Moses is the most important person in Jewish history of the Old Testament." Give at least two reasons for your answer.

Ruth, Naomi, Yochanan ben Zaccai

Students of ancient Hebrews typically will spend much time studying King Solomon, King Saul, King David, Abraham, Sarah, and Moses. However, Ruth, Naomi, and Yochanan ben Zaccai are also important Hebrew figures. Read these brief summaries and answer the questions below.

Ruth and Naomi

Ruth was an ancient Moabite. Moabs were enemies of the ancient Hebrews. Ruth lived in Moab territory and married a Jew. After her husband's death, she converted to Judaism. Naomi, Ruth's mother-in-law, was living in Moab territory but decided to return to Israel after her son died.

Naomi told Ruth to stay with her people, the Moabs. Ruth replied, "Wherever you go, I will go. Wherever you lodge, I will lodge…Where you die, I will die." (Ruth 1:16) In Jerusalem Naomi arranged for Ruth to marry, and a descendant of Ruth was King David.

Yochanan ben Zaccai

When Romans invaded Jerusalem and began to murder all Jews and destroy the Jewish temple, Rabbi Yochanan ben Zaccai offered surrender to Roman general Vespasian, if the general would grant Zaccai one request. The rabbi said, "Give me Yavneh (a city with a great university), and all its sages (professors, philosophers, and religious leaders). Partly because of Rabbi Yochanan ben Zaccai's actions, many Jews lived through this hard time, and the Jewish faith remained alive up to today.

Questions

1. Who were Ruth and Naomi? <u>Naomi: Jewish mother-in-law of Ruth, a Moab</u>

2. What is the story of these two women? <u>After Ruth's husband died, Naomi went back to live with Hebrews. Ruth followed her, even though Moabs were enemies of Hebrews.</u>

3. What do the actions of Ruth and Naomi tell you about friendship of the ancient Hebrews? <u>For ancient Hebrews, friendship and family were extremely important.</u>

4. How did Rabbi Yochanan ben Zeccai save many Jewish lives, and perhaps save the Jewish faith? <u>He made a deal with General Vespasian to save a Jewish university and professors. The deal worked.</u>

5. What do the actions of Rabbi Yochanan ben Zeccai tell you about the character of the ancient Hebrews? <u>Ancient Hebrews were clever and had forethought in dealing with militarily stronger adversaries.</u>

Early Hebrew Leaders

Early Hebrew leaders helped build a faith that has lasted approximately 4,000 years. What was the role of each? Was one leader more important than another? Following the directions of your teacher, research these early Hebrew leaders and decide, from your research, which one played the greatest role in the early Jewish faith.

Early Hebrew Leaders
Importance for Hebrews?
Abraham: God spoke to Abraham first. He told Abraham he would have a son, and commanded him to move to a promised land. Abraham and his wife Sarah had Isaac, who became the beginning of the Jewish people. Abraham led his people to the Promised Land.
Moses: Moses was raised as a prince in ancient Egypt. Moses returned to his people, the Hebrews, and lived as a shepherd. He rescued the Jews out of Egyptian slavery, crossed the Red Sea, and wandered with the Jews for 40 years in the wilderness until reaching the Promised Land. This is called the Exodus.
King David: As a boy, David's faith in God led him to bravely fight and defeat a giant named Goliath. David went on to become a mighty Hebrew king. King David built the city of Jerusalem and made it his capital.
King Saul: Saul was the first ancient Hebrew king. He defeated many enemies in battle. After failing to completely destroy an enemy tribe as God's prophet Samuel had instructed him to, Saul lost God's anointing. Saul committed suicide in a battle he was losing.
King Solomon: King Solomon is the builder of the great Hebrew temple in Jerusalem. Solomon is known for his wisdom to know good and bad. Solomon had great wealth, made many alliances, and ruled a peaceful land. At his death, though, his kingdom split in two. The Old Testament explains that it was Solomon's polygamy and tolerance of paganism that caused his kingdom to split.
Naomi: See previous page.
Ruth: See previous page.
Yochanan ben Zaccai: See previous page.

A Brief History of Early Judaism

Research key events in early Jewish history and detail who was most prominent in them. Which Jewish leaders were the most important during these key events?

Key Events for Ancient Hebrews	
Key Event	**Who? What?**
1. God reveals himself to man	1. God told Abraham to move to Canaan from Ur in about 1900 B.C. Jews, Christians, and Muslims believe Abraham and Sarah to be their ancestors.
2. Exodus: flight from Egypt	2. Moses leads the Hebrews out of their slavery in Egypt and they wander for 40 years in the desert wilderness.
3. God makes a covenant with man	3. God tells the Hebrews through Moses they are God's people. God provides the Hebrews with a set of laws.
4. A Jewish kingdom begins	4. A kingdom was established in the Promised Land under King Saul. King David chooses Jerusalem as the capital.
5. Temple of Jerusalem is built	5. King Solomon makes the Hebrew Kingdom powerful and wealthy. He builds a huge temple at Jerusalem.
6. Romans destroy Jerusalem	6. In A.D. 66, Romans destroy Jerusalem, leaving only the Western Wall of the Temple.
7. Jews disperse to the world (Diaspora)	7. Jews escape Roman persecution by scattering to various parts of the world.

Defend or reject: Moses was the most important Hebrew of the Old Testament.

_____
_____
_____
_____
_____
_____
_____
_____
_____
_____

Socratic Discussion and Reflection

When you share ideas with other students, your ideas may be reinforced, rejected, or slightly changed. Listening to your classmates' ideas will help you form your own judgment. Write your Reflection from the discussion.

_____
_____
_____
_____
_____
_____
_____
_____
_____
_____
_____
_____
_____
_____
_____
_____
_____
_____
_____
_____
_____
_____
_____
_____
_____
_____
_____

Week Three: Ancient Greece

Paraphrasing

Paraphrasing means to take information from your research and to put it in your own words. This is an important skill to have when writing a research paper. If you copy directly from a source, such as a book, but do not place the words in quotation marks and write the author's name, it is called **plagiarism**. Plagiarism is against the rules of writing and your teacher will not accept the work!

Here is an example of paraphrasing a quote from a teacher.

Quote:
"China's mountainous geography made it very difficult for Chinese leaders to unify their country."
Paraphrase:
Ancient Chinese leaders had a hard time unifying their country because of the many mountains in China.

Practice
Quote:
"Confucius lived in a time of turmoil in China. He wrote about respecting parents and authority. Many Chinese grew to believe in what Confucius wrote about."
Paraphrase:
_____
_____
_____

Quote:
"The Chinese were great traders with other cultures. The Silk Road ran from China through central Asia to the Middle East. Along this trail, Chinese met with Arabs, Africans, Europeans, and other Asians."
Paraphrase:
_____
_____
_____

Socratic Discussion Open-Ended History Question
Greek Governments

Ancient Greece has been called the birthplace of Western civilization, because this culture is the beginning of many ideas and practices of the Western world. Along with new ideas in art, architecture, and science, Greece developed and practiced a variety of political systems. A political system is the way a country is organized. Another way of saying this is the word "government." Ancient Greece is the birthplace of many forms of government.

Research the variety of governments in ancient Greece. After your studies, answer the question "Which government of ancient Greece was the best?" Make your answer as convincing as possible.

Types of Government in Ancient Greece

In ancient Greece, from about 1500 B.C. to 146 B.C., Greek city-states experimented with many different types of government. In one type, one man would rule the entire city and would make important decisions. In another city a group of men would rule. And in another city many men made decisions. During these years, it seems nearly all of the world's different kinds of governments existed at one time or another.

In this activity, define the type of government that is listed. Ancient Greece practiced these different governments. After you have defined the governments, decide which government sounds best to you and explain why.

Types of Government in Ancient Greece

Type of Government	Define
1. Monarchy	1. A king has ultimate power. When he dies, his son takes over.
2. Oligarchy	2. This word means "rule by a few." A small group of men rule a society.
3. Tyranny	3. One person has ultimate power, usually for life.
4. Democracy	4. Citizens vote for their leaders, and citizens can become leaders. Every few years there are elections.

Question: Which type of government seems best to you? Why?_____
_____
_____
_____

Voices of Ancient Greece

Read how ancient Greeks thought about the different forms of government. Think about their words. What do they say about democracy and tyranny? Pericles was a politician and Herodotus a historian.

I. Democracy
Pericles (460 B.C. - 429 B.C.): "When it is a question of settling private disputes, everyone is equal before the law; when it is a question of putting one person before another in positions of public responsibility, what counts is not membership of a particular class but the actual ability which the man possesses."
Write this in your own words: All men are created equal. Nobody has special privileges. The best candidate for public office should serve because he is the best. Who holds political power should not depend on who has the most money or the most important family name.
II. Tyranny
Herodotus (c. 430 B.C.): "They became decidedly the first of all. These things show that, while undergoing oppression, they let themselves be beaten, since then they worked for a master; but so soon as they got their freedom, each man was eager to do the best he could for himself."
Write this in your own words: When men are being oppressed, they do not do the best they can, but they lose to others. But when men are free, they will fight and do the best they possibly can. Freedom brings out the best in man.

Question: Which system of government seems better, according to these two Greek authors? What reasons do they give?_____
_____
_____
_____
_____

Socratic Discussion and Reflection

When you share ideas with other students, your ideas may be reinforced, rejected, or slightly changed. Listening to your classmates' ideas will help you form your own judgment. After the class discussion, write down your answer to the question, "Which government of Ancient Greece was best?" Explain which civilization is responsible for the contributions you choose, and explain how these contributions are important to us today.

_____
_____
_____
_____
_____
_____
_____
_____
_____
_____
_____
_____
_____
_____
_____
_____
_____
_____
_____
_____
_____
_____
_____
_____
_____
_____
_____
_____
_____

Week Four: The Hellenistic Age
Socratic Discussion Open-Ended History Question
Was Alexander the Great Really Great?

Questions on Alexander the Great

1. How did the Hellenistic Age differ from the Hellenic Age? <u>In the Hellenistic Age, Greeks did not owe their allegiance to the city-state. Kingdoms and empires became the new organization as opposed to the city-state.</u>

2. What was the new avenue to the good life in the Hellenistic Age, according to the Greek philosophers? <u>Freedom from the emotional stress was viewed as the new way to the good life, according to Greek philosophers.</u>

3. Under the Hellenistic Age, what did Greeks start to think of people that was different than in the Hellenic Age? <u>In the Hellenistic Age, Greeks began to view people as part of the world, and not just either Greek or barbarian. Greeks began to develop universal truths for all mankind.</u>

4. Who was Alexander's tutor? <u>His tutor was Aristotle, one of Greece's most important philosophers.</u>

5. Where did Alexander conquer? <u>He conquered the Persian Empire, Egypt, and nearly all of Greece.</u>

6. How did Alexander bring East and West closer together? <u>He conquered much of the East, he married a Persian bride, he made 80 Greek officers and 10,000 Greek soldiers marry Near Eastern women, and founded Greek cities.</u>

7. What was the greatest result of Alexander's conquests? _____
_____
_____
_____
_____
_____
_____
_____
_____
_____
_____
_____
_____
_____
_____
_____
_____
_____
_____

Socratic Discussion and Reflection

When you share ideas with other students, your ideas may be reinforced, rejected, or slightly changed. Listening to your classmates' ideas will help you form your own judgment. After the discussion, write your reflection.

_____
_____
_____
_____
_____
_____
_____
_____
_____
_____
_____
_____
_____
_____
_____
_____
_____
_____
_____
_____
_____
_____
_____
_____
_____
_____

Week Five
Roman Republic and Roman Empire
Socratic Discussion Open-Ended Question
The Roman Republic

Not enough can be said of the Roman Republic, which existed from 509 B.C. to 60 B.C. Its government was the model American Founders used to create the United States of America in 1789. Roman laws became the framework of legal systems in many countries, such as France, Great Britain, Spain, and the United States of America. The language of Rome is the ancestor of all romance languages, such as Portuguese, Spanish, French, and Romanian. Roman architectural structures are still in use today. Without a doubt, understanding the Roman Republic is essential to understanding Western civilization.

While there is no debate about the greatness of the Roman Republic, there are questions of what led to the success and its downfall. Was it the government, the laws, the architecture, the army? Answer the questions "What are the two most important causes of the greatness of the Roman Republic? How was Rome great?

In your answer, know these terms as they relate to the Roman Republic and Empire:

Republic	Romulus and Remus	architecture
tribunes	veto	branches of government
Twelve Tables	Cincinnatus	written constitution
Roman Law	dictator	Roman army

Republic

A **government** is a group of people who lead a country. In the Roman Republic, the government was a republic. A **republic** is a government where citizens vote for representatives who govern. Founders of the United States of America looked to the ancient Romans for ideas on how to govern. From 1775-1789, Thomas Jefferson, Benjamin Franklin, John Adams, James Madison, George Washington and others formed our government. These men did not want to have a king, but they could not find an example of a government in the world where there wasn't a king or a dictator. American Founding Fathers looked back over 2,000 years to the Roman Republic for ideas. Because of this, the government of the United States looks very much the same as the government of the Roman Republic.

In this activity, research how the government of the Roman Republic was formed, and notice how similar it is to the government of the United States of America.

Government of the United States of America		
1. Congress	**2. President**	**3. Courts (Judges)**
Makes the law	Enforces the law	Interpret the law
Who chooses leaders of government in the U.S.A.? Citizens of the U.S.A.		

Government of the Roman Republic		
1. Roman Assemblies	**2. Consuls**	**3. Praetors (Judges)**
Makes the law	In war - dictator	Interprets the law
Who chose leaders of government in the Roman Republic? Citizens of the Roman Republic		

Questions: Fill in the blanks above with answers to these questions.
1. Who made law in the Roman Republic?   The Senate
2. Who enforced the law in the Roman Republic? Consuls; in war, Dictator
3. Who interpreted the law in the Roman Republic? Praetors
   (interpret means to say if the law is fair or not)
4. Who chose leaders of government in the Roman Republic? From 509 B.C. to 287 B.C., only patricians chose leaders. After, all citizens (patricians and plebeians) chose leaders.
5. How is the American government similar to the Roman government? All citizens choose leaders, and there are three branches of government.

Socratic Discussion Open-Ended Question
The Fall of the Roman Empire

Ancient Roman civilization is arguably one of the most important societies for the Western world. Roman contributions in language, law, art, architecture, religion, and other facets of life are still felt in countries such as France and the United States. During its zenith, the Roman Empire spanned as far west as Britannia, east into Asia, north into present-day Germany, and south into Africa. It is hard not to overstate Roman influence in the development of Western civilization.

Like many great civilizations ancient Rome fell. The Western Roman Empire finally collapsed in A.D. 476. (The Eastern Roman Empire, known as Byzantium, continued until A.D. 1453)

Based on the evidence you research, what were the two most important reasons for the fall of the Roman Empire?

Reasons for the Fall of the Roman Empire

1. In A.D. 395, the empire permanently split into two separate entities. This was one reason the Western Roman Empire fell in A.D. 476.
2. German barbarians attacked the Roman Empire.
3. Asian Huns attacked the German barbarians and the Roman Empire.
4. The Romans became more concerned with their riches than with strength.
5. German general Odoacer conquered Rome in A.D. 476.
6. Roman mercenaries didn't care about the Roman Empire.
7. Criminal gangs broke laws and robbed merchants.

Explain Your Reasons for the Fall of the Roman Empire

1. The two empires split resources and became weaker.
2. German barbarians were stronger than the Roman Empire.
3. Asian Huns pushed German barbarians west into the Roman Empire.
4. Romans didn't work hard and let their empire get weak.
5. If your capitol is conquered, your country usually loses.
6. A mercenary is somebody who fights for money, and might not fight the best.
7. When crime overtakes a society, the society gets weak.

Rating the Reasons for the Fall of the Roman Empire

Reasons for the Fall	Rating (1-10)*		Reason for the rating
1. Split in two	1.	3	1. West and East didn't cooperate
2.	2.		2.
3.	3.		3.
4.	4.		4.
5.	5.		5.
6.	6.		6.
7.	7.		7.
*A score of 1 means this reason is the most important.			

Socratic Discussion and Reflection

When you share ideas with other students, your ideas may be reinforced, rejected, or slightly changed. Listening to your classmates' ideas will help you form your own judgment. After the class discussion, write your reflection.

_____

_____

_____

_____

_____

_____

_____

_____

_____

_____

_____

_____

_____

_____

_____

_____

_____

_____

_____

_____

_____

_____

_____

_____

Week Six: Christianity
Socratic Discussion Open-Ended Question
Christianity

The birth of Jesus Christ in an animal stable over 2,000 years ago heralded the beginning of the world's largest religious belief, Christianity. Approximately 33 years after this birth, the Roman governor in Palestine Pontius Pilate ordered this man to be put to death on a cross. From such small beginnings started the religious belief with over two billion believers in our present day.

From its beginning, Christianity has been a persecuted religion. Followers of Christ were tortured and fed to gladiatorial animals in the Roman circus by the Roman Emperors. However, as time went on, the relationship between the Christian Church and the Roman Empire changed.

Answer the question "Why did the Roman Empire change from persecuting Christians at the time of the death of Jesus to supporting Christians by the Fourth Century?"

In your answer, you should be familiar with these terms:

Messiah	Jesus Christ	New Testament	St. Paul	St. Peter
Apostle	Trinity	resurrection	salvation	Pope
Constantine	Theodosius	missionary	Gentile	

What is Christianity?

In this activity you will research the basic facts and beliefs of Christians. Using your textbook or readings provided by your teacher answer these questions.

Christianity
1. When did Christianity begin? Christians believe the birth of Jesus Christ fulfilled an ancient prophecy of the Messiah coming, sometime near the beginning of the calendar.
2. How did Christianity begin? Jesus Christ was born, preached and crucified.
3. What does it mean to be a Christian? To be a Christian means to be "Christ -like." Christ is the example for all Christians.
4. What is the primary book for Christians? The New Testament
5. What did the Old Testament say about a Messiah? Prophets of the Old Testament foretold a savior that was coming into the world.
6. For a Christian, what does salvation mean? Salvation means unity with the Holy Trinity in heaven and salvation from eternal damnation in hell.
7. Who was Peter? Peter (also known as Saint Peter) was one of the twelve apostles of Jesus Christ. Catholics believe he was the first leader, or Pope, of the Christian Church.
8. Who was Paul (also known as Saint Paul) and what did he do? Saint Paul was a zealous Jew who persecuted Christians. He had a conversion and became a Christian missionary.
9. How did Christianity spread throughout the Roman Empire? Christians spoke about Christianity, traveling throughout the Empire. Christians believe miracles and Christ-like behavior persuaded others to become Christians.
10. What is your opinion of Christianity?

Paraphrase: Here is a quote from Jesus in the New Testament (John 15:13) "No one can have greater love than to lay down his life for his friends." In your own words, write what Jesus said: _____

Change over Time

Change over time refers to the idea that people, countries, groups, knowledge, and just about everything change over time. As students of history we should be aware of this idea of change. We should be able to analyze these changes and decide how the changes affect people. Just think how much the invention of the car changed how people travel. Similarly, imagine a life where our society would still have slavery. To understand change in societies is important as a historian.

For this exercise, research and write how the relationship of the Roman Empire with Christianity changed from the death of Jesus to the year A.D. 395.

Questions

1. Who was Saul of Tarsus, and how did he change his mind about Christians? <u>Christians believe Saul was an ardent Jew who persecuted Christians. He had a conversion experience and became a Christian missionary.</u>

2. What did Saint Paul do to spread Christianity? <u>St. Paul traveled throughout the Roman Empire and spoke about Jesus Christ.</u>

3. According to tradition, how did Saint Peter and Saint Paul die? <u>It is believed the Roman government executed both St. Peter and St. Paul. It is believed by some Christians St. Peter was crucified upside down, and St. was beheaded.</u>

4. What did the Roman Emperor Nero (A.D. 64) do to Christians when he blamed Christians for setting fire to Rome? <u>Nero killed Christians by crucifixion, burning to death, or gladiatorial games.</u>

5. What did the Roman Emperor Decius (A.D. 250) order his soldiers to do to Christians who refused to worship Roman gods? <u>Emperor Decius ordered his soldiers to kill Christians who refused to worship Roman gods.</u>

6. What did Emperor Constantine do in A.D. 313 that was good for Christians? <u>Emperor Constantine issued the "Edict of Milan," giving Christianity equal rights with other religions in the Roman Empire.</u>

7. What did Emperor Theodosius declare in A.D. 395 regarding the Christian faith? <u>Emperor Theodosius declared the Christian faith to be the state religion of the Roman Empire.</u>

Socratic Discussion and Reflection

When you share ideas with other students, your ideas may be reinforced, rejected, or slightly changed. Listening to your classmates' ideas will help you form your own judgment. After the class discussion, write your reflection.

_____
_____
_____
_____
_____
_____
_____
_____
_____
_____
_____
_____
_____
_____
_____
_____
_____
_____
_____
_____
_____
_____
_____
_____
_____
_____

Week Seven: Ancient India
Socratic Discussion Open-Ended Question
Ancient India and the Caste System

In about 1500 B.C. Aryans invaded the Indus Valley and took over much of northern India. The Aryans, a group of warriors and herders, brought with them their way of religion, language, and political culture. The Aryans believed in many gods and had a book of religious writings called The Upanishads. Aryans spoke a language called Sanskrit. In addition, the Aryans had a political and social way of life called the caste system.

The Aryans were so successful in their invasion and conquering of India that many aspects of their way of life stayed in India until the 1950s. For about 3,500 years India had the caste system that the Aryans had brought with them. Answer the question "Do you think that the caste system was fair to everyone in society? Why or why not?" In your answer, make sure you describe the caste system in detail.

What is the Caste System?

The Caste System	
Class	**Role in Society?**
1. Brahmins, or priests	1. Provide spiritual leadership
2. Rulers and warriors	2. Lead and defend from enemies
3. Vaisya	3. Landowning Farmers, merchants, craftsmen
4. Sudra	4. Laborers
Below the Caste System	
1. In ancient India there was one group below this caste system. Which group was so low it wasn't part of the caste system? The lowest group was called *pariahs*, or *Dalit* or *untouchables.*	
2. What was its role in society? These were scavengers, poor farmers, or sanitation workers.	
3. How could a person move up or down to a different class? Moving from one caste to another was virtually impossible. Some believed you could be reborn into a higher caste if you lived a good life.	
Questions	
1. What do I think of the caste system? _____	
2. Would I like to live in a place with a caste system? Why or why not?_____	
3. When and how did the caste system officially end in India?_____	

Socratic Discussion Open-Ended Question
Hinduism and Buddhism

Two of the world's great religions have their birthplace in India. Buddhism and Hinduism are religions professed by many people of Asia and around the world today. Originating approximately 2500 years ago, these religions share some characteristics.

Research the basic beliefs and practices of Buddhism and Hinduism. Learn how these two religions are similar and how they are different. Compare and contrast Hinduism and Buddhism. Show two ways that these religions are similar and two ways they are different.

Hinduism
1. When did Hinduism begin? Somewhere between 1500 and 1300 B.C.
2. What is the name of the main book Hindus read for religious instruction? The Vedas.
3. What is dharma?   This means something like individual ethics, and also way of the Truths.
4. What is karma?   It is the idea, that how you live today will affect what kind of life you will have when you are reincarnated.
5. Did ancient Hindus believe in the caste system? Yes
6. Do Hindus believe in reincarnation (dying, and then being born into the world again)? Yes
7. Do Hindus believe in one God, more than one god, or any god? Hindus believe there is one God, although there appears to exist lesser gods.
8. What is the goal of someone who is a Hindu? The goal of a Hindu is to live a good life and be united with Brahma, the world soul.
9. How does a Hindu reach this goal? Hindus practice spiritual devotion, service to others, and strive for knowledge and meditation.
10. What is your opinion of Hinduism? Each student will have his own answer.

Buddhism
1. When did Buddhism begin? Between 563 B.C. and 483 B.C.
2. How did Buddhism begin? It began from the experiences and teachings of Siddhartha Gautama, known as "Buddha."
3. What does the term "the Buddha" mean? Buddha means "The Enlightened One."
4. What are the Four Noble Truths, according to Gautama Buddha? 1. All worldly life is painful and full of sadness. 2. Desire for pleasure and possessions cause suffering. 3. When you rid yourself of desire, you have reached nirvana and the end of suffering. 4. By following the Middle Way, you can reach nirvana.
5. What is the Middle Way? This is an eight-step guide to good conduct, good thoughts, and good speech.
6. Do Buddhists believe in reincarnation (dying, and then being born into the world again)? Buddhists believe this is possible, but try to avoid this.
7. Do Buddhists believe in one god, more than one god, or any god? Buddhists don't believe in one God like Jews, Christians, or Muslims.
8. What is the goal of someone who is a Buddhist? The goal is to reach nirvana by following the eightfold path.
9. How does a Buddhist reach this goal?   Basically, one gives up searching for pleasures and possessions of the world, be kind and unselfish, study, and be pure thought, action, and speech.
10. What is your opinion of Buddhism? _____

Compare and Contrast

To **compare** means to look at two or more objects and recognize what they have in common. To **contrast** means to look at two or more objects and recognize what they have different from each other.

Compare and contrast Buddhism with Hinduism.

BUDDHISM AND HINDUISM		
Buddhism		**Hinduism**
Differences	Similarities	Differences
1. nirvana	1. reincarnation	1. continual reincarnation
2. one Founder-Buddha	2. ancient religions	2. founders - Aryans
3. be kind to all	3. try to live a good life	3. caste system
4. eightfold path	4. transcendental truth	4. four objectives
5. Not one almighty God	5. originated in India	5. One main God

Socratic Discussion and Reflection

When you share ideas with other students, your ideas may be reinforced, rejected, or slightly changed. Listening to your classmates' ideas will help you form your own judgment. After the class discussion, write your reflection.

_____
_____
_____
_____
_____
_____
_____
_____
_____
_____
_____
_____
_____
_____
_____
_____
_____
_____
_____
_____
_____
_____

Week Eight: Ancient China
Socratic Discussion Open-Ended Question
Unifying Ancient China

China has one of the world's oldest civilizations, beginning about 4,500 years ago. As in all early civilizations, geography was a key factor as to where the first settlements began. The first Chinese societies started near the rivers of the Yellow, the Yangtze, and the Hsi. These early societies would later develop into the great Chinese dynasties.

One of the greatest tasks Chinese leaders had was in unifying all the Chinese in one government. Answer the question "What made unifying ancient China so difficult?"

Calligraphy

Calligraphy is a Chinese way of writing. Instead of letters, which represent sound, in calligraphy small pictures represent whole words and ideas. Calligraphy was introduced to ancient China in the Shang period, over 3,500 years ago. Before calligraphy, Chinese could not communicate well with each other throughout all of China.

Written language was very important to China, as it made it possible for all Chinese people to communicate with each other. In ancient China, each Chinese settlement had a different way of speaking the Chinese language. These differences, called dialects, made it hard for people from different cities and villages to communicate with each other. Since calligraphy had pictures, which represented whole words or ideas, all Chinese could communicate with this new written language.

Chinese Writing – Calligraphy

Research calligraphy. Try to draw Chinese symbols in the boxes below. Write underneath what your symbol represents.

Geography of China

Take out a map of China, which shows deserts, mountains, and rivers. Imagine you are a very powerful and aggressive military leader who lived 4,000 years ago in China. Answer the following questions about the geography of China. After you have answered the questions, try to imagine yourself setting out with a strong army in ancient China to unify the country. What would be the most challenging aspect to unify China?

Questions:

1. By looking at a map, how would you describe China? China is very mountainous and has large deserts and a large coastline.
2. What mountain range is to the southwest of China? The Himalayas are to the southwest of China.
3. Where is the largest mountain in the world located and what is its name? The largest mountain in the world is Mount Everest (29,017 feet, 2 inches) marks the border between Nepal and China.
4. What mountain range is in the north of China?   Altay mountains are in the north of China.
5. What desert is to the northwest of China? The Gobi Desert is to the north and the Takla Makan Desert is to the west of China.
6. Name the major rivers of China and describe where they are. The Hwang Ho River is in the north of China; the Yangtze River is in central China; the His River is in the south of China.
7. Are there mountains all throughout China? Almost throughout all of China are mountains.
8. Would mountains make it difficult to conquer a country? Why or why not? It is difficult to conquer a mountainous country because it is challenging to move an army across and because it was difficult to communicate across mountains.
9. Would rivers make it difficult to travel in ancient China? Why or why not? Rivers made it easier to travel. It is easier for a boat to sail than a person or animal to walk.
10. What do you think might be the most challenging part of unifying ancient China? The many mountains and large deserts made it challenging to communicate between different regions. Also, none of the major rivers flow north to south or south to north.

Socratic Discussion Open-Ended Question
Confucianism

Ancient China was arguably the world's most advanced civilization. Possibly the greatest philosophers of China lived in the fifth and sixth centuries B.C. Philosophers of ancient China taught that people should respect peace, honor families, be dutiful, and have good behavior. Two such philosophers were Confucius and Lao-tzu. This essay will focus on Confucius.

Confucius (551-479 B.C.) is sometimes called China's first philosopher and first teacher. The time in which Confucius lived was marked by much violence between kings and nobles. Confucius taught his students through short sayings how to have a peaceful society. After he died his students wrote these sayings down in a book that is called Lunyu in Chinese and The Analects in English.

Read a small collection of Confucius' sayings on the following page. After reading, answer the following question. "For a society to be strong and peaceful, which two of these sayings do you think are most important?" Paraphrase these two sayings and explain why you think a society should follow these ideas.

Paraphrase Writings of Confucius

Paraphrase the following quotations by Confucius. On your own, research more words of Confucius.

1. "Before you embark on a journey of revenge, dig two graves."
Paraphrase: _____
_____

2. "Forget injuries. Never forget kindnesses."
Paraphrase: _____
_____

3. "He who will not economize will have to agonize."
Paraphrase: _____
_____

4. "The superior man, when resting in safety, does not forget that danger may come. When in a state of security he does not forget the possibility of ruin."
Paraphrase: _____
_____

5. "When anger rises, think of the consequences."
Paraphrase: _____
_____

6. "I am not one who was born in the possession of knowledge; I am one who is fond of antiquity, and earnest in seeking it there."
Paraphrase: _____
_____

7. "Hold faithfulness and sincerity as first principles."
Paraphrase: _____
_____

8. "If a man withdraws his mind from the love of beauty, and applies it as sincerely to the love of the virtuous; if, in serving his parents, he can exert his utmost strength; if, in serving his prince, he can devote his life; if in his intercourse with his friends, his words are sincere - although men say that he has not learned, I will certainly say that he has."
Paraphrase: _____

Most Important Sayings

Rate the importance of the quotes on the preceding page for a society to be strong and peaceful and explain why you gave the verses this rating. A rating of 1 means "most important."

Quote #	Rating (1-4)	Reason for this Rating

Quote #	Rating (1-4)	Reason for this Rating

Quote #	Rating (1-4)	Reason for this Rating

Quote #	Rating (1-4)	Reason for this Rating

Socratic Discussion and Reflection

When you share ideas with other students, your ideas may be reinforced, rejected, or slightly changed. Listening to your classmates' ideas will help you form your own judgment. After the class discussion, write your reflection.

_____
_____
_____
_____
_____
_____
_____
_____
_____
_____
_____
_____
_____
_____
_____
_____
_____
_____
_____
_____
_____
_____
_____
_____
_____
_____

Week Nine: The Middle Ages in Europe
Socratic Discussion Open-Ended Question
Medieval Europe

Medieval Europe generally means the period of history from the fall of the Roman Empire (A.D. 476) to the beginning of the Modern Age (c. 1500). During this time, medieval Europeans developed political systems, religion, and ways of living that would lead Europe into a prominent position in the world. Two institutions, the Crown (which the king represents) and the Roman Catholic Church (which the Pope represents) battled over political power.

Answer the question "Who held more political power in the medieval ages in Europe, the Crown or the Roman Catholic Church?" Defend your answer using sound evidence.

You should be familiar with the following names and terms:

medieval monasteries	feudalism	Papacy	monarch
Charlemagne	Emperor Henry IV	Magna Carta	Islam
habeas corpus	Judaism	Crusades	interdict
excommunication	Catholic Church	St. Thomas Aquinas	

Monarchism in Medieval Europe

Politics is the art or science of governing, or ruling. In looking at the different groups in a medieval society and comparing their political power, you can decide how important politics was in the everyday life of a medieval European. Did the political rights of a person determine how he lived, how he thought, and how he acted? Because Europe has so many countries, and because primarily the English founded the U.S.A., we will look at English monarchy in the year 1295 to fill in this graphic organizer.

Title of the Ruler of England

King

Members of Parliament

Members of Parliament from the House of Lords and the House of Commons

Poor Farmers Who Had No Say in Politics

Serfs

Questions:

1. What was the title of the ruler of England in 1295? The King
2. Which group(s) of English society was represented in Parliament in 1295? The nobility
3. In 1295, who had no political power in England? The Serfs
4. Did the king have any power or control over the Catholic Church in 1295? It is debatable whether the king had more power over the Church in 1295.
5. Was there ever an event in English medieval ages where a king acted violently against a leader of the Catholic Church? What happened? King Henry II encouraged his guards to kill the highest-ranking church official in England, Archbishop Thomas Becket. The guards killed the Archbishop.

Feudalism in Medieval Europe

Economics is how a person, or society, makes, sells, and distributes commodities (stuff). Studying economics helps us understand how people bought and sold items, and how people farmed and got food on the table. While working on this page, think how important a role economics had in the daily life of a medieval person.

Leader

| 1. King |

Large, Powerful Landowners

| 2. Nobility | | 2. Nobility |

Warrior Class

| 3. Knights | 3. Knights | 3. Knights |

Poor Farmers Who Worked the Land

| 4. Serfs |

Questions:

1. Who was the supreme leader of the land? (In chess, his wife is very powerful.) The King
2. Who were the landlords of medieval farm property? The Nobility
3. Who promised to fight a certain number of days a year in return for land? Knights
4. Who were not allowed to move from the property they farmed and were the lowest class in medieval society? Serfs
5. Could somebody from the Catholic Church, such as a priest or a bishop, own land and also be a knight or a lord? Yes

Power Struggles: The Crown and the Roman Catholic Church

Here are two examples of a power struggle between kings and the Catholic Church during the European Middle Ages (476–1500). Use your textbook and logical thinking to fill in the blanks.

King Henry IV (1056-1106) and Pope Gregory VII

King Henry IV and Pope Gregory VII disagreed over who should have the power to <u>choose</u> bishops and priests. The king and the Pope <u>both</u> wanted the power. Because King Henry IV would not follow the Pope, Gregory VII <u>excommunicated</u> the king. English nobles and bishops would not support the King, because they were <u>afraid</u> of excommunication. King Henry IV traveled to the Vatican <u>barefoot</u> during winter to show the Pope his humility. The King had to wait <u>three</u> days outside before the Pope would see him and accept his <u>apology.</u> The king and Pope then signed the <u>Concordat</u> at Worms (1122), ensuring that only the <u>Pope</u> had the power to choose bishops and priests.

Church	**choose**	**apology**	**both**	**excommunicated**
Concordat	**afraid**	**barefoot**	**three**	

King Henry II (1154-1189) and Archbishop Thomas Becket

English King Henry II got into an argument with <u>Archbishop</u> Tomas Becket about the **power** of the king. Becket fled England for France. When Archbishop Becket was in <u>France,</u> King Henry II wanted Prince Henry crowned as king, but only Archbishop Becket had the power to do this. King <u>Henry</u> II had other church leaders crown Prince Henry as king. Archbishop <u>Becket</u> came back to England and <u>excommunicated</u> the bishops who had crowned Prince Henry. King Henry II got very <u>mad</u>, yelled in rage, and four of his knights went immediately to Archbishop Becket and <u>hacked</u> him to pieces in a cathedral. As punishment, the Pope made Henry build three monasteries and send 200 soldiers on the Crusades.

excommunicated	**Archbishop**	**Henry**	**France**
Becket	**mad**	**hacked**	**power**

Question:

1. Did the Pope or the King have more power in medieval England? What evidence do you have that supports your answer?_____

_____

_____

_____

Socratic Discussion and Reflection

When you share ideas with other students, your ideas may be reinforced, rejected, or slightly changed. Listening to your classmates' ideas will help you form your own judgment. After the class discussion, write your reflection.

_____

_____

_____

_____

_____

_____

_____

_____

_____

_____

_____

_____

_____

_____

_____

_____

_____

_____

_____

_____

_____

_____

_____

_____

_____

_____

Week Ten
The End of Medieval Civilizations

Open-Ended Socratic Discussion Question
St. Thomas Aquinas

Did St. Thomas Aquinas correctly explain how faith and reason are compatible?

Open-Ended Socratic Discussion Question
Spread of Christianity

In Medieval Europe, did Christianity spread more because of leaders like Charlemagne or because of Christian missionaries such as St. Benedict of Nursia, St. Patrick of Ireland, St. Boniface, St. Cyril and St. Method?

Open-Ended Socratic Discussion Question
Ancient, Middle, and Modern Ages

What are the main differences between the Middle Ages and the Modern World? What is the difference between the Ancient World and the Middle Ages?

Socratic Discussion and Reflection

When you share ideas with other students, your ideas may be reinforced, rejected, or slightly changed. Listening to your classmates' ideas will help you form your own judgment. After the class discussion, write your reflection.

_____
_____
_____
_____
_____
_____
_____
_____
_____
_____
_____
_____
_____
_____
_____
_____

Week Eleven: Islamic Civilizations
Socratic Discussion Open-Ended Question
Contributions of Islamic Civilization

In the seventh century A.D., one of the world's most important religions emerged on the Arabian Peninsula. Muhammad, a seventh-century Arab, began the religion of Islam, whose followers are called Muslims. Muslims call Muhammad the Prophet and they believe that there is one God, Allah. By Muhammad's death in A.D. 632, many of the people of Arabia were Muslim. In the next 120 years Muslims spread their religion through Asia, North Africa, and Spain.

Medieval Islamic civilizations contributed much to the world in the areas of science, geography, mathematics, philosophy, medicine, art, literature, and through trade. Based on your research, what were two of the greatest contributions Muslims made to world civilizations?

Medieval Islamic Contributions

Contribution	Description
1. The religion of Islam	1. A monotheistic religion
2. Zero and Arabic numerals	2. Important math concept
3. Poetry	3. Omar Khayyam - author
4. Improvement of Algebra	4. Important math concept
5. Ibn Sina wrote medical encyclopedias	5. Important for medicine

Importance of Contributions Today

How is this contribution important today?
1. Islam is one of the world's largest religions.
2. The world uses the zero and Arabic numerals.
3. A society that produces poetry contributes to literature.
4. Algebra is used in math, science, space, and elsewhere.
5. Medical encyclopedias spread knowledge that saves lives.

Rating of Contributions

Rating, in order of importance	Reason for rating
1.	1.
2.	2.
3.	3.
4.	4.
5.	5.

Socratic Discussion Open-Ended Question
Muhammad and Jesus Christ

Compare and contrast Muhammad with Jesus Christ.

Socratic Discussion Open-Ended Question
Spread of Islam

How did Islam spread during its first three hundred years? Did it spread mainly through military conquest or religious persuasion?

Socratic Discussion Open-Ended Question
The Crusades

Were the Arab Muslims correct to conquer the Holy Land? Were the Christians correct to try to take back the Holy Land four hundred years later?

Socratic Discussion and Reflection

When you share ideas with other students, your ideas may be reinforced, rejected, or slightly changed. Listening to your classmates' ideas will help you form your own judgment. After the class discussion, write your reflection.

_____
_____
_____
_____
_____
_____
_____
_____
_____
_____
_____
_____
_____
_____

Week Twelve: Medieval China and Medieval Japan
Socratic Discussion Open-Ended Question
Medieval China

Medieval China was arguably the world's most advanced and strongest civilization. The first two great medieval Chinese dynasties, the Tang and the Sung, made China a leading civilization. The dynasties of Tang (A.D. 618–907) and Sung (A.D. 960–1279) are known for great agricultural, technological, medical, mathematical, academic, literary, and commercial developments. In time, Chinese inventions and techniques would spread throughout the world.

Research the greatest contributions that the Chinese made to world civilizations in the Tang and Sung period. Using this research, answer the question "What were the two most important Chinese contributions to world civilizations during the Tang and Sung dynasties?" Explain your choices in detail.

Tang Dynasty (A.D. 618–907)

Tang contribution	Describe what it was and how it was important
1. Printing	1. A quick way to copy books - ideas spread
2. Encyclopedias	2. Books of knowledge – knowledge spread
3. Women civil servants	3. Women could work in government – freedom
4. Sculptures	4. Rock sculptures for religious worship
5. Poetry	5. Cultural life flourished

Sung Dynasty (A.D. 960–1279)

Sung contribution	Describe what it was and how it was important
1. Small pox inoculation	1. Medicine to prevent deadly disease – saved lives
2. Invention of abacus	2. Adding machine – made it easier to count
3. New Weapons	3. Weapons that used gunpowder
4. Printing invention	4. Invention that made more books available to all
5. Painting	5. Culture creates a richer society

Prioritize the Contributions
Place the contributions in order of importance to the world.

Contribution	Describe what it was and how it was important
1.	1.
2.	2.
3.	3.
4.	4.
5.	5.

The Words of Marco Polo

In 1295, Marco Polo returned to Venice after living and working in China for 25 years. Although he experienced China under a Mongol leader, Kublai Khan, Marco Polo witnessed the advanced society that the Tang and Sung dynasties had created. While in a jail cell in Genoa (a city in present-day Italy), he shared his experiences with Rustichiello, a writer. Rustichiello wrote the stories of Marco Polo, and these stories spread throughout Europe. Below is an account by Marco Polo of a city of China.

> "Inside the city there is a Lake which has a compass of some 30 miles and all round it are erected beautiful palaces and mansions, of the richest and most exquisite structure that you can imagine, belonging to the nobles of the city…In the middle of the Lake are two Islands, on each of which stands a rich, beautiful and spacious edifice, furnished in such style as to seem fit for the palace of an Emperor. And when any one of the citizens desired to hold a marriage feast, or to give any other entertainment, it used to be done at one of these palaces.

Polo, Marco, "The Glories Of Kinsay [Hangchow] (c. 1300")", From The Book of Ser Marco Polo the Venetian concerning the Kingdoms and Marvels of the East, trans. and ed. by Henry Yule, 3rd ed. revised by Henri Cordier (London: John Murray, 1903), Vol II. Pp. 185-193, 200-205, 215-216,

Paraphrase
To the best of your ability, paraphrase the above quote

_____
_____
_____
_____
_____
_____
_____
_____
_____
_____
_____
_____
_____
_____
_____
_____
_____
_____

Medieval Japan

From A.D. 1185 to 1867 powerful military generals named "shoguns" ruled Japan. These shoguns attempted to keep the peace among warring Japanese. The samurai, or warrior class, controlled large areas of land and taxed peasants. Samurai received their land from the shogun, or from larger landholders called daimyo, when the samurai promised loyalty and service.

Answer the question "What kind of society did the shoguns create in Japan? Under the Shoguns, was Japanese society open or closed, peaceful or violent, culturally rich or culturally barren?" You should be familiar with the following names and terms:

shogun daimyo samurai   Japan   Minamoto Yoritomo

Feudalism   Ashikaga   Buddhism   Francis Xavier Tokugawa

This essay has six assignments:

Feudalism in Japan

Leader without Power

1. Emperor

Chief Military General
(Head of Finances, Courts, and Government)

2. Shogun

Large, Powerful Landowners

3. Daimyo		3. Daimyo

Warrior Class

4. Samurai		4. Samurai		4. Samurai

Poor Farmers Who Worked the Land

5. Peasants

Feudalism in Medieval Japan

Answer the questions and fill in the flow chart above.
1. Who held the most important title? The Emperor
2. Who was actually in charge of the country? The Shogun
3. Who were large, powerful landowners? The Daimyo
4. Who were the warriors who received land for promising loyalty? The Samurai
5. Which people were at the very bottom of Japanese society? The Peasants
6. Source of information:

Japan under Shoguns: Open or Closed?

When a society is open, its citizens are free to learn, discuss, and accept ideas or customs from foreign countries. A closed society rejects outside ideas. The time of the shoguns was A.D. 1185–1867. Using your book, fill in the missing pieces to the table below.

Place of Origin	What?	When?	Accepted?
1. Korea	Buddhism	500s	Yes
2. China	Chinese Writing	400s	Yes
3. Europe	Christianity	1500s	No
4. China	Zen Buddhism	1300s	Yes

5. Source: In what book, and on what pages, did you find the information? _____

Question: Based on your research for this activity, do you think Japanese society under the shoguns (A.D. 1185–1867) was open or closed? What evidence do you have that supports your judgment?_____

_____

_____

_____

_____

_____

Japan under Shoguns: Peaceful or Violent?

The different shoguns of Japan are listed below. Research if they were peaceful or violent. Make your decision for each and write brief notes that support your judgment.

Kamakura Shogunate (1192–1333)	Peaceful or Violent? (evidence?) Japan defended itself against Kublai Khan (1274).
Ashikaga Shogunate 1568)	Peaceful or Violent? (evidence?) (1333– Civil War took place in Japan in the late 1400s until 1603.
Civil War (c. 1568–1603)	Peaceful or Violent? (evidence?) General Hideyoshi tried to invade Korea and China.
Tokugawa Shogunate (1603–1867)	Peaceful or Violent? (evidence?) No major wars occurred. European Christian missionaries were killed.

Question: Overall, in judging the three shogunates, do you think the shogun era in Japan was peaceful or violent? What evidence do you use to prove this?_____

_____

_____

_____

_____

Culturally Rich or Culturally Barren?
Medieval Japan 1185–1867

One definition of culture is "intellectual and artistic ideas, thoughts, and words and the works produced by these." In judging for yourself whether medieval Japan had a rich cultural life, you will research Japanese intellectual and artistic activities and decide on your own if these activities are enough to say that medieval Japan was culturally rich or culturally barren.

Note to the teacher: This is only a very short list of Japanese cultural life.

Literature & Poetry	List and briefly describe Japanese works
	"Noh" plays are classical musical dramas. were produced in Bunraku is puppet theatre. Kabuki is a traditional theatre.

Art	Briefly describe Japanese art:
	Artistic tea ceremonies were practiced in Japan. Origami originated in medieval Japan. Japanese painting and calligraphy developed in medieval Japan.

Artistic Gardens	Describe:
	Artistic Japanese gardens consist of intricate rock designs and delicate flower arrangements such as ikebana.

Dance	Describe:
	The Bon dance is performed to remember ancestors. The Buyo dance is a mixture of dance and pantomime.

Question: Was medieval Japan culturally rich or culturally barren? What evidence do you have that supports this judgment?_____
_____
_____
_____

Socratic Discussion and Reflection

When you share ideas with other students, your ideas may be reinforced, rejected, or slightly changed. Listening to your classmates' ideas will help you form your own judgment. After the class discussion, write your reflection.

_____
_____
_____
_____
_____
_____
_____
_____
_____
_____
_____
_____
_____
_____
_____
_____

Week Thirteen: Medieval Africa
Socratic Discussion Open-Ended Question
Medieval Africa

The power of the medieval African empires of Ghana and Mali rested in part on the business of trading. Africans traded with Arabian Muslims gold, salt, food, slaves, copper, and weapons. Because of this trade, the Arabic language and the Islamic religion spread in Africa. Also, the African empires of Ghana and Mali were able to trade for needed products, such as salt. Ghana and Mali became two of the richest empires in Africa, and perhaps in the world.

One product the Africans traded to the Muslims was the slave. Usually prisoners of war or criminals were used as slaves. In modern society in the United States, we view slavery as an evil. In Africa and in much of the world in the medieval ages, though, it was seen as normal. Answer the question "What were the two most important reasons Africans traded Africans as slaves?"

Trading in Medieval Africa

Items Traded	
From Ghana and Mali to Arabia	**From Arabia to Ghana and Mali**
1. Gold	1. Salt
2. Ivory	2. Copper
3. Slaves	3. Cloth
4. Leather	4. Tools
5.	5.

Islamic Influence in Africa

Because of the trans-Saharan caravan trading between Africa and Arabia, Africa adopted many religious and cultural characteristics of Arabia. List the ways how Islamic Arabia influenced and changed Africa.
1. Some Africans became Muslims.
2. Mosques were built in Africa.
3. Trade brought wealth to cities and kingdoms in Africa.
4. Some African kings based their laws on the Koran.
5. Arabs brought a system of writing to Africa.

Questions

1. What did Ghana and Mali trade to Arabia? _gold, slaves, leather, ivory_
2. What did Arabia trade to Ghana and Mali? _salt, copper, cloth, tools_
3. Did Ghana and Mali receive Arabian items needed for survival? If so, what item(s)? _Salt_
4. Did medieval Africa benefit from the trans-Saharan trade? How or how not? _Yes, because it brought medieval Africa wealth. No, because some Africans became slaves._
5. What did Arabians and Africans think about slavery? Did they think buying and selling humans was wrong, right, normal, or abnormal? _Africans and Arabians thought buying and selling humans as slaves is correct and normal._
6. What does the Koran say about slavery? _The Koran states that slavery is allowed._
7. What does the Koran say about enslaving non-Muslims? _The Koran states that it is the right of Muslims to enslave those captured during war and that that Muslims may make wives of women captured in war._
8. Did Muhammad own slaves? _Yes._

Socratic Discussion and Reflection

When you share ideas with other students, your ideas may be reinforced, rejected, or slightly changed. Listening to your classmates' ideas will help you form your own judgment. After the class discussion, write your reflection.

_____

_____

_____

_____

_____

_____

_____

_____

_____

_____

_____

_____

_____

_____

_____

_____

Week Fourteen: The Renaissance
Socratic Discussion Open-Ended Question
The Renaissance

In the early medieval ages up to the fourteenth century (1300), European civilization lagged behind Asian and Middle Eastern cultures in areas such as medicine, science, and trade. However, this was soon to change. From A.D. 1300 to 1700, Europeans greatly changed many aspects of their lives. Amazing advances were made in the arts, cartography, trade, technology, and science. This time period is known as the Renaissance, which is a French word for "rebirth." It describes a rebirth of interest in classical arts, classical literature, and a great desire to discover.

Answer the question "During the time of the Renaissance in Europe (A.D. 13001700), what three aspects of life changed the most?" Use these terms and names correctly in your answer, showing you understand their meaning and significance to the Renaissance.

the arts	philosophy	trade	religion	science
mathematics	cartography	anatomy	astronomy	Dante
da Vinci	Guttenberg	Shakespeare	exploration	humanism
Silk Road	Michelangelo			

Change over Time

Change over time refers to the idea that people, countries, groups, knowledge, and just about everything changes during a period of time. As students of history, we should be aware of changes, and we should be able to analyze and see how these changes affect people. Just think how much the invention of the car changed how people travel! Or, imagine a life where our society would still have slavery. To understand change in societies is important as a historian.

For this exercise, list the term you researched and write very briefly how it changed from 1300 to 1700. Then rate how big of a change this was on a scale of 1 to 10, 10 being the biggest change. The first two are done for you. (Of course, don't include the names of people!)

Term	Change	Rate
1. the arts	1. Art focused more on human beauty and realism.	1.
2. philosophy	2. Humanists trusted human intellect more.	2.
3. trade	3. Trade exploded between Europe and the world.	3.
4. religion	4. The Christian Church broke apart.	4.
5. science	5. Scientific method established; discoveries made.	5.
6. cartography	6. "New" continents mapped.	6.
7. anatomy	7. The human body was dissected and mapped.	7.
8. exploration	8. North and South America discovered.	8.
9. Guttenberg	9. His printing press made spread of ideas easier.	9.
10. humanism	10. Human endeavor became the center of thought.	10.

Preparing your Position

Choose three of the terms that you rated as the most changed during the Renaissance. List these terms in the space provided below and include all of the evidence you have that supports your judgment. In your essay, you will list the items that you rated lower and include the evidence that shows these changes were less important.

1. Change:
Evidence:

2. Change:
Evidence:

3. Change:
Evidence:

Socratic Discussion and Reflection

When you share ideas with other students, your ideas may be reinforced, rejected, or slightly changed. Listening to your classmates' ideas will help you form your own judgment. After the class discussion, write your reflection.

_____

_____

_____

_____

_____

_____

_____

_____

_____

_____

_____

_____

_____

_____

Week Fifteen: The Reformation
Socratic Discussion Open-Ended Question
The Reformation

Since the time Christians believe Jesus Christ walked the earth (c. A.D. 4) for over 1500 years there had been one major organized Christian church in Europe, the Roman Catholic Church. In sixteenth - century Europe, however, many Christians were upset with the Roman Catholic Church for reasons of faith, corruption, and personal gain. Some Christians tried to change the Church from within, but others formed new churches. The Christian churches that formed were known as "Protestant" because believers were "protesting" the Catholic Church.

Two major Protestant reformers were Martin Luther and King Henry VIII. These men found so much support against the Catholic Church that they founded new religions, the Lutheran Church and the Anglican Church. Compare and contrast the reasons Martin Luther and King Henry VIII had in founding new religions.

Be familiar with these terms and people in your essay:

Ninety-five theses	salvation	divorce	indulgences
Excommunication	Act of Supremacy	Tudor	Protestant
Church of England	Counter-Reformation	corruption	

Compare and Contrast

To **compare** means to look at two or more objects and recognize what they have in common. To **contrast** means to look at two or more objects and recognize what they have different from each other.

For this assignment, fill in the chart below to help you compare and contrast. Under "Martin Luther" and "King Henry VIII," write how the two men differed in their conflicts with the Roman Catholic Church. Under "Similarities," write what the men had in common in their protest against the Church.

Martin Luther		King Henry VIII
Differences	**Similarities**	**Differences**
Former Catholic Priest	Men of important position	King of England
Married a former Catholic Nun	Married	Married 6 times
Protested Catholic Church because of Catholic abuses.	Started a new religion	Protested Catholic Church because he wanted to remarry.
German	European	English
Sparked religious wars	Caused religious wars	Executed Catholics
Started Lutheran Church	Started a new religion	Church of England (Anglican Church)

Socratic Discussion and Reflection

When you share ideas with other students, your ideas may be reinforced, rejected, or slightly changed. Listening to your classmates' ideas will help you form your own judgment. After the class discussion, write your reflection.

_____

_____

_____

_____

_____

_____

_____

_____

_____

_____

_____

_____

_____

_____

_____

Week Sixteen
Absolutism, The Age of Exploration, The Commercial Revolution
Socratic Discussion Open-Ended Question
The Age of Exploration

From the 1400s through the 1600s, European countries embarked on amazing journeys of exploration and discovery throughout the world. Known as "The Age of Exploration," Portugal and Spain led Europe in discovering the Americas, opening up Asia further for trade, and paving the way for colonization of the New World. People from other continents did not fully participate in this age of exploration.

In your essay, answer the questions "What were the two most important causes of the Age of Exploration? Why did Europeans lead in the Age of Exploration and people from other continents did not take part?" In your answer, list and briefly describe the great voyages of exploration. Also, research these terms to help determine your answer:

Renaissance	spices	Asia	Italy	Dias
Vasco de Gama	Columbus	Magellan	Cabot	Jamestown
Portugal	Spain	France	England	Holland
Enlightenment	Prince Henry the Navigator			

Cause and Effect

Cause and effect is a term that means one event made another event happen. For example, if you push against the pedals of your bicycle, the bicycle moves. In this example, the push against the pedals is the cause and the bicycle moving is the effect.

CAUSE -------------------------------→EFFECT
push against pedals--------------→bicycle moves

In social studies, cause and effect usually relates events and people. The relationship is trickier to understand than the above example with the bicycle. Sometimes it is difficult to see causes and effects in history. Write down the cause on the left. In the middle, write the effect of each cause. Then rank the most important causes of the Age of Exploration 1 to 10 with 1 being the most important. .

Term (Cause)	Effect	Rank
1. Search for Spices	1. Europeans built good ships.	
2. Crusades	2. Europeans introduced to the world.	
3. Desire for Gold	3. Europeans searched the world.	
4. Missionary Zeal	4. Europeans spread Christianity.	
5. Spaniards beat Moors	5. Spaniards felt very confident.	
6. English Corporation	6. English could raise money to support exploration.	
7. Renaissance	7. Europeans were eager to discover.	
8. Absolute Monarchs	8. European kingdoms could raise money.	
9.	9.	
10.	10.	

Socratic Discussion and Reflection

When you share ideas with other students, your ideas may be reinforced, rejected, or slightly changed. Listening to your classmates' ideas will help you form your own judgment. After the class discussion, write your reflection.

_____
_____
_____
_____
_____
_____
_____
_____
_____
_____

Week Seventeen: The Scientific Revolution and the Age of Enlightenment
Socratic Discussion Open-Ended Question: The Scientific Revolution

For over 1400 years, the western mind had accepted writings of ancient Greek, Roman, and religious writers to explain not only religious thought but science and nature as well. Then, within the next 200 years, a radical change took place. Instead of accepting ancient writings on science and nature without question, western philosophers and scientists strove to experiment and observe what really exists. The results of this change in thought and action were incredible. We call this change "The Scientific Revolution." The Scientific Revolution affected how the western mind thought, believed, and acted.

Answer the question "Which three changes in thought or action were the most important in the Scientific Revolution, from 1500–1800?" Describe the Scientific Revolution and identify the most important individuals and breakthroughs in this time period. Your answers may be a specific discovery, an invention, an idea/theory, or anything else that is relevant.

Be familiar with these terms in your essay:

Scientific Revolution	scientific method	Copernicus	Galileo
Kepler	Newton	telescope	thermometer
barometer	Bacon	Descartes	John Locke
Andreas Vesalius	William Harvey		

Rate the Change

List the terms you have researched, and briefly describe the change. Then rate the importance of this change with "1" meaning the most important change, "10" meaning the least important change.

Term /Person	Description of Change	Rating
1. Scientific Revolution	1. Man looked to observation instead of religion for answers.	_____
2. scientific method	2. Experimentation and observation became the method of knowledge.	_____
3. Copernicus	3. Argued that the sun was the center of the universe.	_____
4. Galileo	4. Made a telescope and proved the sun was the center.	_____
5. Newton	5. Put forth the theory of gravity.	_____
6. Bacon	6. Put forth the scientific method.	_____
7. Descartes	7. Placed the human at the center of all.	_____
8. Vesalius	8. Examined dead humans and detailed human body correctly.	_____
9. Harvey	9. Explained how the circulatory system works	_____
10. Locke	10. Wrote that government should mainly protect life, liberty, and property	_____

Socratic Discussion and Reflection

When you share ideas with other students, your ideas may be reinforced, rejected, or slightly changed. Listening to your classmates' ideas will help you form your own judgment. After the class discussion, write your reflection.

_____

_____

_____

_____

_____

_____

_____

_____

_____

_____

_____

Week Eighteen: The French Revolution
Socratic Discussion Open-Ended Question
The Age of Revolution

For most of the medieval ages (c. A.D. 476–1500), Europeans did not question the divine right of kings and queens. Europeans believed that God personally chose their leaders, and therefore following the rulers was both a political and a religious act. In some lands the king exercised absolute power, that is, power without limits.

From the 1600s through the mid-1800s, however, revolution swept through many of the great countries of Europe and its large colonies. Kings were violently deposed from power, in some cases losing their heads in public executions. The era of divine right was forever broken, and the age of revolution heralded new ideologies.

Answer the question "What was the key factor in destroying the idea of the divine right of kings?" Explain what ended the power of the great absolute monarchs and brought in a radically different kind of state.

You should be familiar with the following ideas and terms:

nationalism	absolute monarch	limited monarchy
Enlightenment	self-government	English Bill of Rights
Magna Carta	Declaration of Independence	

Important Documents on the Rights of the Individual

Research the following documents and provide a short summary for each. Then answer the questions at the bottom of the page.

The Magna Carta (1215): This document forced King John I to give up power to the English noblemen. The king had to request tax money from nobles in order to wage war, instead of demanding money. Noblemen also gained property and civil rights.
The English Bill of Rights (1689): All English citizens obtained political rights due to this document.
The American Declaration of Independence (1776): The United States of American declared itself and independent country from Great Britain and declared that all mean are created equal and that the government's job is to protect life, liberty, and the pursuit of happiness.
The French Declaration of the Rights of Man and the Citizen (1789): This document declared that all citizens were equal under the law and rejected privileges for the nobility.
The American Bill of Rights (1791): This document guaranteed American citizens freedoms from their state and federal governments.

1. Did these documents grant more power to the king (or government) or less? Each of these documents takes power away from the king or grants the citizens more rights.
2. Which of the documents guarantees the most individual freedom from government? Each student may have a different answer. Let students explain their answers.

The Enlightenment

Research these philosophers of the Enlightenment and write down their main ideas involving the ideas of good government.

Political Philosophers
John Locke: Englishman John Locke lived from 1632–1704. Locke wrote in the "Two Treatises of Government" that all men have natural rights and that the government's main job is to protect these rights. Natural rights meant the right to life, liberty, and private property.
Thomas Hobbes: Englishman Thomas Hobbes lived from 1588–1679. Hobbes wrote that man gives up some of his rights to an authority so that he may live in a peaceful society. Man enters into a social contract with a government to ensure his own safety and protection.
Charles Louis-Montesquieu: Frenchman Montesquieu lived from 1689–1755. Among other works, he is most famous for his writings on separation of powers. He wrote that it is necessary to place the varied powers of government into the hands of a number of men so that not all powers would reside in one man, or in one group.
Jean-Jacque Rousseau: Franco-Swiss Rousseau lived from 1712–1778. Rousseau believed that man lived as a noble savage until he was constrained by government. Rousseau wrote that a small group of citizens should determine the *general will,* what was best for others. Citizens should be forced to follow this general will.

Economics and the Enlightenment
Research the following economic term and its most known proponent.
Laissez faire: This is a French term which refers to an economic policy where the government leaves business alone. Today, *free market* is more often used.
Adam Smith: Scottish Smith lived from 1723–1790 and wrote "Inquiry into the Nature and Causes of the Wealth of Nations." He remains the most well-known proponent of free trade and perhaps the father of economics.

Questions
1. Did the philosophers of the Enlightenment want a stronger king? Most Enlightenment philosophers did not want a stronger king.
2. Do you think that most kings were in favor of or against philosophers of the Enlightenment? Why or why not?_____ _____

Nationalism

1.	What is nationalism? Nationalism is the idea that the most important aspect of a human is his nationality, that each nation deserves a state, and that all other loyalties a person may have are secondary to the allegiance he holds to his nation.
2.	When did the idea of nationalism become a major factor in European politics? Most historians think that the idea of nationalism became a major factor in European politics at the time of the French Revolution (1789) and Napoleon's reign.
3.	How did Napoleon Bonaparte spread ideas of nationalism in Europe? When Napoleonic France conquered much of Europe, he spread nationalistic ideas. Also, people fighting Napoleon were inspired by nationalistic ideas.
4.	Did the idea of nationalism support having empires controlled by a king from a different nationality? No. The ideology of nationalism supported a king ruling his own nation.
5.	In England, under King Henry VIII, what did the British king do to the Roman Catholic Church? King Henry VIII started
6.	In the German speaking lands, during the life of Martin Luther, describe what was happening in Europe. German nobility were deciding to side with either the Catholics or the Lutherans. Religious wars broke out among Catholics and Lutherans.
7.	Did the Protestant Reformation support the idea of divine right, or weaken it? The Protestant Reformation weakened the idea of divine right. Lutheran German princes fought against the Holy Roman Emperor, who was crowned and legitimated by the Roman Catholic Church.
8.	Did the idea of nationalism make emperors of multinational emperors stronger, or weaker? Why? The idea of nationalism made emperors of multinational empires weaker. One idea of nationalism is that each nation deserves its own country. For the multinational empires, this meant that individual nations within the empire would want to break away and start their own country.

The Age of Napoleon

Napoleon Bonaparte was born and raised on the French-controlled island Corsica. Of lower nobility, Napoleon went to France at the age of 13 to learn how to become a soldier. As a young man and officer in the army, France was in thralls to the French Revolution and the Reign of Terror. During this time, over 40,000 Frenchmen were executed and chaos ruled in France. Peasant revolts swept the countryside and European empires invaded France in an attempt to restore the king. Searching for order and stability, the French turned to Napoleon, who quickly rose to power through his military prowess. Napoleon used the power of the military and his charisma to take over France.

Once in charge of France, Napoleon took the ideals of the French Revolution and brought them to the rest of Europe. The French Revolution was, in part, an attempt to bring great reforms in society. These changes meant to rid Europe of slavery and inequality. By military conquest Napoleon introduced these liberal ideas to the rest of Europe. On one hand, Napoleon promoted the freeing of slaves, suffrage for adult males, and the dissolution of empires that may have discriminated against ethnic minorities. On the other hand, Bonaparte militarily conquered nearly all of Europe, destroying armies and empires and forcing nations either to be part of France or to be its ally.

Discuss the accomplishments and failures of Napoleon and take a stand on this question "Was Napoleon a hero or a villain?" Use sound evidence and logical arguments to defend your thesis.

Be familiar with these terms:

nationalism	the French Revolution	the Enlightenment
empire	constitutional monarchy	Napoleonic Code
Declaration of the Rights of Man	Jacobins	Reign of Terror
King Louis XVI	Napoleonic Wars	

The French Revolution

1. In 1788 France.....
   a. Who was the First Estate? Nobility
   b. Who was the Second Estate? Clergy
   c. Who was the Third Estate? Farmers, laborers, and merchants
   d. Which two estates ruled but represented a small number of French? The First Two Estates ruled but represented only 3% of the population.

2. In 1788 France, did the law treat everyone the same? Did a poor person have the same rights as the king? French law treated people unequally. The king had more rights than a poor person.

3. A society where some people have more rights than others is a society of inequality.

4. Who created the National Assembly and why? The Third Estate called for a National Assembly because this would give more power to the Third Estate.

5. What happened on July 14, 1789, at the Bastille? Why? Parisians rioted and attacked the Bastille fortress, which the king used as a prison. Parisians falsely believed political prisoners were held there. Rioters slaughtered the jailor.

6. What did the Declaration of the Rights of Man state? The Declaration of the Rights of Man stated that all people have the right to free speech, press, and religion. It guaranteed trial by jury and put an end to harsh punishments.

7. Why did Prussia, Austria, and later Britain, Spain, and Holland all attack France? The French Revolution was a threat to all monarchies in Europe. European monarchs wanted to help the French king and queen.

8. Who were the Jacobins and the Committee on Public Safety? The Jacobins were a group of radicals within the National Assembly who wanted to get rid of the king and control France. The Jacobins led the Committee on Public Safety, which was responsible for killing approximately many French citizens in a time known as the Reign of Terror.

9. What happened to King Louis XVI and his wife, Queen Marie Antoinette? The National Assembly found the king and queen guilty of treason and the two were guillotined.

10. In the Reign of Terror, what was life like in France (How many died? Why were they killed? Who was Robespierre)? During the Reign of Terror, the Committee on Public Safety terrorized French society. 30,000 were accused of being against the Revolution and were guillotined, drowned, or shot. Most accusations were false and convictions did not rely on evidence. Maximilien Robespierre led the Jacobins, who led this time of terror. In 1794, Robespierre was beheaded and the Reign of Terror stopped.

11. What ended the French Revolution? The Reign of Terror was ended by a moderate group in the National Convention, but Napoleon Bonaparte ended the French Revolution by taking over the government in 1799.

The Age of Napoleon

I. **The Napoleonic Code:** Once in power, Napoleon ended the French Revolution and the Reign of Terror. Stability and order returned to France. Napoleon created a new set of laws for France, known as the *Code Napoleon*, or the *Napoleonic Code*. This code is still the basis for law in France. Under the code, slaves were freed, and a more equal society was created.

    A. What does this code say about equality of citizens under the law? <u>Citizens are equal under the law.</u>

    B. How does the code deal with religion? <u>Citizens have freedom of religion.</u>

    C. How was the Napoleonic Code different from law under the king? <u>Under the king, nobility and clergy had more rights than commoners. All French had to be Roman Catholic before the Code. The Code provided for trial by jury.</u>

    D. What is a plebiscite and when did the French vote for Napoleon? <u>A plebiscite is an up or down vote for a leader. The French voted for Napoleon in a plebiscite in ???</u>

    E. Do you think the Napoleonic Code was good for France? Why or why not? _____

    F. The Napoleonic Code has been used in many countries, and even in some states in the U.S.A. (such as Louisiana). Did Napoleon positively affect society where his code was adopted? Why or why not? _____

II. **The Napoleonic Wars (1805-1815):** Although under Napoleon stability and order returned, peace did not. France tirelessly waged war on all of Europe.

    A. Napoleon crowned himself the emperor of France. Why didn't he let the Pope crown him? <u>Napoleon wanted to be seen as superior to the Church.</u>

    B. Name the kingdoms that Napoleon conquered. <u>He conquered all or parts of the kingdoms of Austria, Italy, Russia, Spain, and Prussia, Naples, and the Ottomans.</u>

    C. What was the *Continental System*? <u>Napoleon attempted to form a European Empire and conquer Great Britain.</u>

    D. What revolutionary ideas did the French spread when Napoleon conquered other lands? <u>The French outlawed slavery, brought ideas of social and political equality, and promoted religious freedom.</u>

    E. How did Spain react after Napoleon's invasion? <u>As with many countries, Spain fought Napoleon and the French.</u>

    F. What invasion by Napoleon began his downfall? <u>Napoleon conquered much of Russia, but winter and a Russian counterattack beat him.</u>

    G. Which battle was Napoleon's last? <u>Napoleon lost the Battle of Waterloo in Belgium in 1815.</u>

Quotations on the Age of Napoleon

Read the following quotes from Napoleon Bonaparte and briefly describe — based on his words — what type of person he was.

"It is the cause, not the death, that makes the martyr."

"Never interrupt your enemy when he is making a mistake."

"Victory belongs to the most persevering."

"Take time to deliberate, but when the time for action has arrived, stop thinking and go on."

"I have fought sixty battles and I have learned nothing which I did not know at the beginning."

"A Constitution should be short and obscure."

"Death is nothing, but to live defeated and inglorious is to die daily."

"If I had to choose a religion, the sun as the universal giver of life would be my god."

"In order to govern, the question is not to follow out a more or less valid theory but to build with whatever materials are at hand. The inevitable must be accepted and turned to advantage."

_____
_____
_____
_____
_____
_____
_____
_____
_____
_____
_____
_____
_____
_____
_____
_____

Socratic Discussion and Reflection

When you share ideas with other students, your ideas may be reinforced, rejected, or slightly changed. Listening to your classmates' ideas will help you form your own judgment. After the class discussion, write your reflection.

_____

_____

_____

_____

_____

_____

_____

_____

_____

_____

_____

_____

_____

_____

_____

_____

_____

_____

_____

_____

_____

_____

_____

_____

_____

Week Nineteen: The Industrial Revolution
Socratic Discussion Open-Ended Question
The Industrial Revolution

The Industrial Revolution in Western Europe and the United States took place roughly between 1750 and 1900. It is called a revolution because of the dramatic change that took place in people's daily lives. In manufacturing, science, transportation, communication, and the workplace, inventions, discoveries, and new ideas altered how people viewed the world and how they lived.

Discuss the most important changes to society during the Industrial Revolution. In what field did inventions or discoveries cause the greatest change in the everyday life of humans? You may choose from the following list: science, medicine, transportation, agriculture, manufacturing, and communication.

You should be familiar with advances and changes in these areas between 1750 and 1900:

medicine   science   transportation   agriculture

manufacturing   communication   philosophy

The Industrial Revolution

Research the greatest changes of the Industrial Revolution in the following categories.

MEDICINE		
Person	**Invention or discovery**	**Effect on society**
Edward Jenner	Vaccinations	Some diseases were eradicated.
Louis Pasteur	Heating milk kills kils bacteria.	Drinking was safer
Robert Koch	Discovered how germs cause disease	Some germs could be killed with sterilization.
Joseph Lister	Strong chemicals kill germs	Killed germs and made operating cleaner and safer

SCIENCE		
Person	**Invention or discovery**	**Effect on society**
John Dalton	Atoms	Advanced atomic studies.
Michael Faraday	Magnetism produces electricity	Electric generators were created
Wilhelm Roentgen	X ray	Doctors could look inside the body without operating
Marie Curie	Radioactive elements: radium and polonium	Furthered study of radiation

TRANSPORTATION		
Person	**Invention or discovery**	**Effect on society**
Robert Fulton	Profitable steamboat	Travel time on water was shortened.
George Stephens	Train	Travel time on land was shortened.
Karl Benz	Internal combustible motor	Too much to write about
Wilbur and Orville Wright	Airplane	Travel time in the air was created.

AGRICULTURE

Person	Invention/discovery	Effect on society
Jethro Tull	Seed drill	Planted seeds in rows, producing more crops.
Charles Townshend	Crop rotation	More crops were produced.
Cyrus McCormick	Mechanical reaper	This harvested grain quicker.
John Deere	Steel plow	Farmers plowed better.

MANUFACTURING

Person	Invention or discovery	Effect on society
John Kay	Flying shuttle	One person operated a loom and cloth was woven quicker.
James Hargreaves	Spinning Jenny	It spun thread faster than the spinning wheel.
Edmund Cartwright	Power loom	This created textiles quickly.
Eli Whitney	Cotton gin	The cotton gin separated seeds from cotton quickly.

COMMUNICATION

Person	Invention or discovery	Effect on society
Samuel F.B. Morse	Wire Telegraph	Communication over long distances was quick.
Gugliemo Marconi	Wireless telegraph	Communication over long distances was quick, and no wires were needed.
Vladimir Zworyka	Television	Moving pictures could be sent through radio waves.

Reflection

Look over the notes you've taken on the last two pages. Answer the following questions.

1. Based on your notes, in what field did inventions or discoveries cause the greatest change in the everyday life of humans?_____

_____

2. How did inventions or discoveries in this field effect (change) everyday life? _____

_____

_____

_____

_____

3. In what field did inventions or discoveries cause the second-greatest change in the everyday life of humans? _____

_____

4. How did inventions or discoveries in this field effect (change) everyday life? _____

_____

_____

_____

_____

5. Choose one person you think was most responsible for the greatest advancement made during the Industrial Revolution. What did he or she invent or discover, and how did this greatly impact the everyday life of humans? _____

_____

_____

_____

_____

Week Twenty: Thought and Culture

1. In a short paragraph, summarize what is Romanticism.

_____

_____

_____

_____

_____

_____

_____

_____

2. In a short paragraph, summarize what is German Idealism.

_____

_____

_____

_____

_____

_____

_____

_____

3. In a short paragraph, summarize what is "classical liberalism." The author of _Western Civilization_ calls this liberalism.

_____

_____

_____

_____

_____

_____

_____

4. In a short paragraph, summarize what is Nationalism as it was understood in the 18th and 19th century.

_____

_____

_____

_____

_____

_____

_____

_____

Week Twenty-One: Liberalism and Nationalism

Socratic Discussion Open-Ended Question
Were the Revolutions of 1848 a Success or a Failure?

Socratic Discussion Open-Ended Question
Compare and Contrast the Unification of Italy and the Unification of Germany

Socratic Discussion Open-Ended Question
Was Bismarck a Hero, Villain, or Neither?

Socratic Discussion Open-Ended Question
How was Nationalism a Problem in the Hapsburg Empire?
Socratic Discussion and Reflection

When you share ideas with other students, your ideas may be reinforced, rejected, or slightly changed. Listening to your classmates' ideas will help you form your own judgment. After the class discussion, write your reflection.

_____
_____
_____
_____
_____
_____
_____
_____
_____
_____
_____
_____
_____
_____
_____
_____
_____
_____

Week Twenty-Two: Thought and Culture in the 19th Century
Socratic Discussion Open-Ended Questions
Realism and Romanticism

Research five works of art that are from Realists and five from Romantics. Write the names of the works and the artists. If you find the artwork on the internet, print the works out so you can show your classes. Which of the style of art do you prefer? Why?

Positivism

Is Comte's three historical stages the correct way to view man?

Charles Darwin

How did Charles Darwin's theories challenge Christianity?

Does Social Darwinism promote genocide against what Darwin termed the "savage races?"

Does Darwinism support racism?

Secularism

Which of the writers against a traditional understanding of Christianity has the most influence today?

Marxism

Was Karl Marx correct in his interpretation of history and economics?

John Stuart Mill

Compare and contrast John Stuart Mill's arguments with Karl Marx's ideas

Feminism

What were the goals of feminism of the 1800s?

Socratic Discussion and Reflection

When you share ideas with other students, your ideas may be reinforced, rejected, or slightly changed. Listening to your classmates' ideas will help you form your own judgment. After the class discussion, write your reflection.

_____
_____
_____
_____
_____
_____
_____
_____
_____
_____
_____
_____
_____
_____
_____

Week Twenty-Three: The Age of Imperialism
Socratic Discussion Open-Ended Question

In the nineteenth century, major industrialized European countries and the United States colonized much of Africa, Latin America, and Asia. Because of the organizational and economic strength of the industrialized nations, small countries were able to master populations many times their size. In 1850, Great Britain was able to rule a nation of 150,000,000 with only 34,000 British soldiers. British rule in India began in the 1700s — when the British East India Company began controlling large areas of land — and lasted until 1947.

Trace British imperialism in India from the onset of colonization to Indian independence. Show the perspectives of the colonizer and the colonized, paying close attention to the role of leaders and religion in the movements for independence. Compare and contrast the different views on British colonization of India.

You should be familiar with these terms and people:

British East India Company	Sepoy Rebellion	Hindus
Muslims	suttee	nationalism
democracy	famine	racism
Queen Victoria	Mohandas K. Gandhi	passive resistance

(You will need to search for some of the information outside of your book.)

The British in India

1. What was the British East India Company and when did it begin to do business in India? <u>This company made money from trade between Asia, Europe, and North America. It began doing business in 1600 and ruled India until 1857.</u>
2. In the early 1700s, besides Great Britain, what European powers did business in India? <u>Holland, Denmark, Portugal, and France all had colonies in India.</u>
3. List two reasons the British thought they were better than the Indians? <u>The British had better guns and did not believe in the practice of sutee (sati), where Indian widows would burn themselves along with their dead husbands. The British also felt Christianity was superior to Hinduism and Buddhism.</u>
4. Describe the Sepoy Rebellion. <u>The Sepoy, Indian soldiers who fought for the East India Company, rebelled against the British in 1857.</u>
5. Describe the practice of suttee. Why did the British outlaw this in India? <u>Indian widows would burn themselves along with their dead husbands. The British outlawed this practice because Western civilization traditionally held that it is sinful or illogical to commit suicide. It didn't seem fair for the surviving woman to kill herself.</u>
6. What did the British introduce to India that involved transportation? <u>The railroad.</u>
7. In education and medicine, how did the British influence India? <u>Indians learned English and Christianity and the British brought Western ideas.</u>
8. When did Queen Victoria become *Empress of India*? <u>1876.</u>
9. What was the Indian National Congress? <u>The Hindu Indians formed the Indian National Congress to strive for independence from the United Kingdom.</u>
10. What was the Muslim League? <u>The Muslim Indians formed the Indian National Congress to strive for independence from the United Kingdom.</u>
11. When did the British leave India and give her independence? <u>1947.</u>
12. What countries did the British create from India and why? <u>The British created Pakistan for the Muslims and India for the Hindus. Pakistan later became Pakistan and Bangladesh.</u>
13. Read the poem on the following page by Rudyard Kipling, an Englishman born and raised in British India. What can we learn from a poem to help us understand history? <u>A poem can teach us what people's feelings and emotions are about historical events and people.</u>

"The White Man's Burden," by Rudyard Kipling (1865-1936)

1. Take up the White Man's burden--
Send forth the best ye breed--
Go, bind your sons to exile
To serve your captives' need;
To wait, in heavy harness,
On fluttered folk and wild--
Your new-caught sullen peoples,
Half devil and half child.

2. Take up the White Man's burden--
In patience to abide,
To veil the threat of terror
And check the show of pride;
By open speech and simple,
An hundred times made plain,
To seek another's profit
And work another's gain.

3. Take up the White Man's burden--
The savage wars of peace--
Fill full the mouth of Famine,
And bid the sickness cease;
And when your goal is nearest
(The end for others sought)
Watch sloth and heathen folly
Bring all your hope to nought.

4. Take up the White Man's burden--
No iron rule of kings,
But toil of ser and sweeper--
The tale of common things,
The ports ye shall not enter,
The roads ye shall not tread,
Go, make them with your living
And mark them with your dead.

5. Take up the White Man's burden,
And reap his old reward--
The blame of those ye better
The hate of those ye guard--
The cry of hosts ye humour
(Ah, slowly!) toward the light:-
"Why brought ye us from bondage,
Our loved Egyptian night?"

6. Take up the White Man's burden--
Ye dare not stoop to less--
Nor call too loud on Freedom
To cloak your weariness,
By all ye will or whisper,
By all ye leave or do,
The silent sullen peoples
Shall weigh your God and you.

7. Take up the White Man's burden!
Have done with childish days--
The lightly-proffered laurel,
The easy ungrudged praise:
Comes now, to search your manhood
Through all the thankless years,
Cold, edged with dear-bought wisdom,
The judgment of your peers.

1. In this poem, how does Kipling view the Indians? _____
_____

2. How does he view the British as colonizers? _____
_____

3. What do the lines "The silent sullen peoples/ Shall weigh your God and you" mean?___
_____

4. In this poem, is Kipling against British colonization of India or for it? _____
_____

Mohandas K. Gandhi (1869-1948)

1. Where was Gandhi born? <u>Gandhi was born in Porbandar, Gujarat, India.</u>
2. At what age did he marry? <u>He married when he was 13 years old.</u>
3. Where did he study to be a lawyer? <u>He studied to be a lawyer in England.</u>
4. Gandhi worked in South Africa for many years. What was his work there? <u>Gandhi worked for civil rights of Indians in South Africa.</u>
5. What does *passive resistance* mean? <u>Passive resistance means not following laws as a means of changing public policy. It is a way of protest that is nonviolent.</u>
6. What did Gandhi think about British colonization in India? <u>Gandhi grew to think that India should be independent of the United Kingdom.</u>
7. How did Gandhi work to rid India of British occupation? <u>Gandhi motivated Indians to acts of civil disobedience and to boycott British goods.</u>
8. What were two major religions of India in the nineteenth century? <u>Hinduism and Islam.</u>
9. How did people of these two religions get along? <u>There were violent problems between the Hindu Indians and the Muslim Indians.</u>
10. When did India achieve independence from Great Britain? <u>1947.</u>
11. What two countries were created from India and why? <u>Pakistan was created for Muslims and India for Hindus.</u>
12. During his life Gandhi would fast (not eat). What were some reasons for his fasting? <u>Gandhi believed fasting purified the person and when he fasted he received media attention for his political goals.</u>
13. Gandhi is called *Mohatma* in India. What does this mean and why is he called this? <u>*Mohatma* means the *great soul* and he is called this because of his power to influence others to act peacefully for India's independence.</u>
14. From where did Gandhi say he receive his courage? How could he stand up to the British empire without any weapons? <u>Gandhi said he received his courage from great Indians (like Navaroji, Tagore, and Tilak) and from great foreigners (like Jesus Christ, Thorough, and Tolstory)</u>
15. What role did religion play in the life of Gandhi? <u>Gandhi placed great importance on religion and God.</u>
16. What major U.S. figure of the twentieth century studied Gandhi and replicated the strategy of nonviolent protest? <u>Dr. Martin Luther King, Jr.</u>

Socratic Discussion and Reflection

When you share ideas with other students, your ideas may be reinforced, rejected, or slightly changed. Listening to your classmates' ideas will help you form your own judgment. After the class discussion, write your reflection.

_____

_____

_____

_____

_____

_____

_____

_____

_____

_____

_____

_____

_____

_____

_____

Week Twenty-Four
Modern Consciousness
Socratic Discussion Open-Ended Question
Modern Consciousness and World Wars

Did the philosophies of Nietzsche, Bergson, and Sorel contribute to the totalitarian regimes of the 20th century?

Modernism in Art

In chapter 17, key artists of modernism are written about. Research works of art by these modernists and compare them with great works of art from the Renaissance period. Compare and contrast Modernist art with Renaissance art. Which do you prefer? Why?

The Enlightenment in Disarray

Marvin Perry writes that at the turn of the century the ideas of the Enlightenment were in disarray. Was that a good or a bad development?

Socratic Discussion and Reflection

When you share ideas with other students, your ideas may be reinforced, rejected, or slightly changed. Listening to your classmates' ideas will help you form your own judgment. After the class discussion, write your reflection.

_____

_____

_____

_____

_____

_____

_____

_____

_____

_____

_____

_____

_____

_____

_____

_____

_____

Week Twenty-Five: Causes and Effects of World War I
Socratic Discussion Open-Ended Question
Causes of World War I

Can the value of one life be so high that it could start a world war? In 1914, Serbian nationalists shot the future ruler of the Austro-Hungarian Empire, Archduke Francis Ferdinand. This one act started a chain reaction, setting off a series of events that led to the first great catastrophic war of the twentieth century. At the time it was called *The War to End All Wars*, or *The Great War*. President Woodrow Wilson had high hopes this war would make the world "safe for democracy." Unfortunately, World War I became Act I of a terrible play for humanity. In addition, many of the European countries that fought in World War I turned to totalitarian governments after the war.

Discuss and evaluate the causes of World War I. After the Serbs assassinated Archduke Francis Ferdinand, was World War I avoidable? If your research shows you it was avoidable, explain how Europeans could have avoided the death and destruction of this four-year conflict. If you find it was unavoidable, explain your answer.

To answer the question, you should be familiar with these terms and people as they relate to World War I:

nationalism	imperialism	alliances	militarism
balance of power	Pan-Slavism	Pan-Germanism	the Triple Alliance
assassination of Archduke Francis Ferdinand			the Triple Entente
Balkans	First Balkan War	Second Balkan War	

Evaluating Causes

On the chart below, first write all the causes of World War I on the right. (You may have causes that are not found on the assignment page. You may also decide not to use all the terms from the assignment page.) Then rank the causes on the left from 1-10, 1 being the greatest cause and 10 the weakest.

Ranking (1–10)	Causes of World War I

Questions

1. Explain your top three rankings. Why do you think these top three were the greatest causes of World War I?_____

_____

_____

_____

_____

2. After the assassination of Archduke Francis Ferdinand, do you think World War I was avoidable? If so, what could have been done to avoid the war? If you think the war was unavoidable, explain why you think this. _____

_____

_____

_____

Effects of World War I

World War I was a war of incredible and catastrophic scope. This "War to End All Wars" may have caused the Russian Revolution, the rise of Hitler, World War II, and the disillusionment of a generation. For the next 70 years, the effects of World War I could be felt throughout the world. Europe — the continent of Socrates, Euclid, Augustine, Dante, and Aquinas — sparked a war that killed over ten million, wounded over 20 million, and may have led to the enslavement of tens of millions in totalitarian regimes. How could such an advanced culture of countries have created the groundwork for the most violent century of humanity?

Discuss the various aims of world leaders at the Paris Peace Conference. Based on your research, were Woodrow Wilson's aims at the conference visionary or naïve? In your answer, compare and contrast the aims of the world leaders with Wilson's goals.

To answer your question best, you should be familiar with these terms and people:

David Lloyd George (Britain)   Georges Clemenceau (France)

Vittorio Orlando (Italy)   Woodrow Wilson (U.S.A.)

secret treaties   Fourteen Points

the Treaty of Versailles   definitions of "visionary" and "naïve"

Secret Treaties

The winning powers of World War I had created secret treaties among each other to divide up the Central Powers, who had lost the war. According to these treaties, the Ottoman Empire, Germany, and Austria-Hungary were to lose parts of their own territories and at least parts of their colonies. In this section of your prewriting activities, research the secret treaties made by the victorious powers of World War I. The United States, led by President Woodrow Wilson, did not make secret treaties.

Spoils of war is a term that refers, in part, to the property or money that the victors in war receive. Russia, Great Britain, France, and Italy made secret treaties that were to dismember the losing countries. In the following graph, write what was promised the victors of war.

The Spoils of War: the Secret Treaties		
Country	**Leader in 1916**	**Territory Promised in Secret Treaties if Country Won the War**
1. France	1. Clemenceau	1. Alsace and Lorraine from Germany
		2. Portions of the Ottoman Empire in Asia
		3. Portions of German Africa
		4. War Indemnity
2. Great Britain	2. George	1. Portions of Asia Minor
		2. Portions of German Africa
		3. War Indemnity
3. Italy	3. Orlando	1. Trent, Southern Tyrol, Istria, Gorizia and Dalmatia (part of Austria-Hungary)
		2. Portions of German Africa
		3. War Indemnity
4. Rumania	4. Bratianu	1. Portions of Austria-Hungary
5. Japan	5. Count Okuma	2. Guarantee of Chinese independence
6. Russia	6. Tsar Nickolas I	1. Portions of the Ottoman Empire in Europe and Asia
		2. Portions of Germany and Austria-Hungary (Russia dropped out of the war early)
7. Serbia	7. Pasic	1. Portions of Austria-Hungary

Question
Based on these secret treaties between the World War I victors, describe the aims of these leaders at the Paris Peace Conference.

Woodrow Wilson's Fourteen Points

When President Woodrow Wilson attended the Paris Peace Conference after World War I, he came with a plan for Europe and the world that he called "the Fourteen Points." In this prewriting activity, research the main ideas of the Fourteen Points, and think how these ideas compare with the secret treaties of the victorious European leaders of World War I.

Main Ideas of Wilson's Fourteen Points	
Main Ideas	Explanation
1. Freedom of the seas	1. The oceans will be open for every country to use without threat of violence.
2. No secret treaties	2. Countries will not make secret treaties.
3. Arms reduction	3. Countries will not build up their militaries.
4. League of Nations	4. Countries will meet regularly to discuss problems before wars break out.
5. Self-determination and nationality	5. Nations will have their own country and people will choose their own leaders.

Questions

Compare and contrast the secret treaties with Woodrow Wilson's Fourteen Points.

1. Based on these main ideas of Wilson's Fourteen Points, describe this president's aims at the Paris Peace Conference in a sentence or two. President Wilson aimed to attack the causes of World War I by spreading democracy, promoting dialogue among countries, and lowering militarism.

2. How did Wilson's aims differ from the other leaders' aims at the Peace Conference? Generally, other leaders wanted to take all that they could from the losers.

3. Which plan — the secret treaties or Wilson's Fourteen Points — do you think would do more for world peace? Explain. _____

_____

_____

Socratic Discussion and Reflection

When you share ideas with other students, your ideas may be reinforced, rejected, or slightly changed. Listening to your classmates' ideas will help you form your own judgment. After the class discussion, write your reflection.

_____

_____

_____

_____

_____

_____

_____

_____

_____

_____

_____

_____

_____

_____

Week Twenty-Six: Totalitarianism
Socratic Discussion Open-Ended Question
The Rise of Totalitarianism

The period between the end of World War I and the onset of World War II was a time of great instability, world depression, and disillusionment of republican values in the great powers of Germany, Italy, and Russia (Soviet Union). Totalitarian governments emerged in these societies and threatened not only Europe, but the entire world as well. *Fascism* and *communism*, though enemies to each other, were two types of totalitarian systems which shared many traits.

Trace the origins of fascism and communism. Compare and contrast these two totalitarian regimes in terms of political philosophy, their aggressive nature, and cost in human lives.

You should be familiar with these terms and people as they relate to the rise of totalitarianism:

fascism	communism	world depression (1930s)
totalitarianism	Vladimir Lenin	Josef Stalin
Adolf Hitler	Benito Mussolini	Weimar Republic
human rights	Russian Revolution	Karl Marx

The Rise of Communism

1. What are the main points of *The Communist Manifesto* (1848) by Karl Marx and Robert Engels? <u>The system of capitalism is morally wrong because owners of capital oppress the city workers. The workers do not receive the fruits of their labor. All workers should be owners in the companies they work in. History is a science that is moving toward a communist world, where capitalism will not exist.</u>

2. What kind of government did Russia have in 1916? <u>Russia had a monarchy.</u>

3. What were the problems in Russia in 1916? <u>Russia was losing many lives in World War I, famine was widespread, and Russians were upset with monarch Czar Nicholas II.</u>

4. Who were the Bolsheviks and when did they take over Russia? <u>The Bolsheviks were the main Communist Party in Russia that took over by force in November 1917.</u>

5. In 1920, who were the top two Bolsheviks in Russia? <u>Vladimir Lenin Leon Trotsky,</u>

6. Under Vladimir Lenin, Russia reorganized into a federation. What was the new name of the country? <u>The Union of Soviet Socialist Republics (U.S.S.R.)</u>

7. In the Soviet Union what freedoms were denied? What could people not do, nor say, that they could in the United States? <u>People could not practice religion, speak against the government, read anything critical against the government, read any literature the government didn't like, choose where they wanted to live, choose their job, travel freely inside and outside the country, listen to many kinds of music, and start businesses.</u>

8. What did the Communists do to private property and to Church property? Why? <u>Russian Communists took private property and Church property and made it state property, because they believed property should be owned by all through the state.</u>

9. After Lenin died who took over in the Soviet Union? <u>Joseph Stalin</u>

10. What was *The Five-Year Plan*? <u>*The Five-Year Plan* was a government-organized set of goals and methods to increase production and improve the economic system in the U.S.S.R.</u>

11. How many civilian lives were killed because of communism? <u>Estimates fall somewhere in between 60,000,000 to 130,000,000.</u>

12. The Soviet Union is known as the world's first modern totalitarian state. Why was it called totalitarian? <u>The state controlled nearly every facet of the individual's life.</u>

13. How long did the Communists remain in power in the Soviet Union? <u>Communist control in the U.S.S.R. ended in 1989.</u>

14. In a Communist state, who or what is more important — the state or the individual? <u>The state</u>

15. Does communism continue the tradition of Western political thought, begun by the Greco-Roman and Judeo-Christian cultures? How or how not? _____

_____

_____

_____

_____

The Rise of Fascism

1. What problems did Italy have after World War I? <u>Italians were upset at not winning much land after the war and they were in the middle of an economic depression.</u>

2. Who was the leader of the Fascists in Italy and what name did he give himself? <u>Benito Mussolini called himself "Il Dulce," meaning "The Leader."</u>

3. From whom did the Italian Fascists claim they were protecting Italy? <u>Italian Fascists claimed they were saving Italy from the Communists.</u>

4. How did Mussolini seize power in Italy? <u>Mussolini and his Fascists beat up and killed people who didn't like him. He led a march on Rome, where many Italians joined him. The democratic government quit before there was a fight, and the king asked Mussolini to be the premier.</u>

5. Who controlled businesses and employees in Fascist Italy? <u>Business leaders controlled businesses in Fascist Italy with close cooperation with the government.</u>

6. What was the Lateran Treaty? <u>This treaty made the Vatican City an independent country and the pope promised to remain neutral in international relations.</u>

7. Who or what was more important in Fascist Italy, the state or the individual? <u>The state</u>

8. After World War I, what economic problems did the first democratically elected government in Germany, the Weimar Republic, have? <u>World War I victors forced Germans to sign the Versailles Treaty that ended World War I. The Treaty made Germany pay World War I victors money, Germans lost land to the victors, and Germany was not allowed an army. Germany was also in a severe economic depression.</u>

9. After World War I, which countries occupied parts of Germany? <u>France, Denmark, Poland, Czechoslovakia, Lithuania</u>

10. Under the Weimar Republic, Germany had to admit *war guilt* for World War I and pay war reparations to the victors of WW I. How did this make Germans feel? <u>Germans were upset because all countries shared in the guilt for the war, not just Germany.</u>

11. What was the shorter name for the *National Socialist German Worker's Party* in Germany? <u>Nazis</u>

12. What is a scapegoat? How did Hitler and the Nazis use the Jews as a scapegoat for Germany's problems? <u>A scapegoat is somebody you place blame on, even though the person or group is not responsible for the blame. Hitler said the Jews were the fault of all of Germany's problems.</u>

13. What did Hitler write about the German race (sometimes he called it the Aryan race)? <u>Hitler wrote the German race was superior to all others in the world.</u>

14. How did Hitler and the Nazis seize power in Germany? <u>The Nazis won the largest percentage of the 1932 vote, 33%. German President Hindenburg made Hitler chancellor. Hitler convinced the other political parties to give him law-making powers through the *Enabling Act*. Hitler then outlawed opposing political groups.</u>

15. How many civilian lives were killed because of fascism? <u>From 12 – 20 million.</u>

16. Does fascism continue the tradition of Western political thought, begun by the Greco-Roman and Judeo-Christian cultures? How or how not? _____

Socratic Discussion and Reflection

When you share ideas with other students, your ideas may be reinforced, rejected, or slightly changed. Listening to your classmates' ideas will help you form your own judgment. After the class discussion, write your reflection.

_____

_____

_____

_____

_____

_____

_____

_____

_____

_____

_____

_____

_____

_____

_____

Week Twenty-Seven: Causes of World War II
Socratic Discussion Open-Ended Question
World War II—Causes of Appeasement

World War II has been the largest and most tragic war of human history. Over 20.5 million civilians were murdered, 12.5 million soldiers were killed, and over 23 million soldiers were wounded. It was a war in which armies targeted whole civilian populations. The German army attempted to exterminate all Jews in the world, and it killed over 6 million, along with 5 million people Nazis deemed subhuman. Germany, Italy, Japan and the Soviet Union invaded and brutalized smaller nations, while the western, democratic countries slowly geared up for war. Consequences of this war can still be seen today in world conflicts, borders, attitudes, treaties, and many other ways.

Before World War II, the western democracies had a number of opportunities to stop or slow down the aggressors. However, throughout the 1930s, Germany, Italy, and Japan were able to get their way. Answer the question "What were the two main causes that led democratic leaders of the world to follow a policy of appeasement towards Adolf Hitler and Benito Mussolini?"

You should be familiar with these terms and people.

appeasement	the Munich Conference	Joseph Stalin
World War I	isolationism	pacifism
Axis Powers	Holocaust	Benito Mussolini
Eastern Europe	Czechoslovakia	Poland
Spanish Civil War	F.D. Roosevelt	Great Depression
Munich Conference (1938)	Winston Churchill	Allies
General Tojo		

Events Preceding World War II

1. The Treaty of Versailles was one of the peace treaties that ended World War I. What in the Treaty of Versailles did not seem fair to Germany? Germany lost land to the victors, could not keep an army, and had to admit war guilt and pay the victors money.

2. Describe Kristallnacht. Did European countries protest against Germany after Kristallnacht happened? Did the United States protest against Germany? On November 9 and 10, 1938, Nazi gangs beat up and killed Jews, destroyed Jewish businesses, destroyed synagogues, and Germany jailed over 26,000 Jews. Foreign countries complained against Kristallnacht, but did not act strongly against Germany.

3. Adolf Hitler used the Jews in Germany as a scapegoat, an excuse for all of Germany's problems. What did Hitler write about the Jews in his book *Mein Kampf?* Hitler wrote that Jews were a disgrace to humans, that Jews only cared about survival, and that Jews were the reason for all of Germany's problems.

4. Name two ways in which Hitler defied (went against) the Treaty of Versailles before 1937. Hitler created a large German army and sent the German army into the Rhineland.

5. During the Spanish Civil War, which countries sent much military support to Spain? Which side won in the war? Mussolini and Hitler sent military help to the National Socialist Franco and the Soviet Union sent aid to the Republicans.

6. What was the *Anschluss* (annexation) of Austria? In 1938, Germany took Austria.

7. a) What was the *Munich Conference* in 1938? Leaders of Germany, Italy, France and the United Kingdom discussed how to make Hitler happy. Germany was allowed to take western Czechoslovakia. Hitler promised he wouldn't take more of Europe.
b) What did the British prime minister announce after these talks? Prime Minister Neville Chamberlain announced that , "Peace for our time."

8. Who did Italy attack in 1936? What did the League of Nations do in response? Italy attacked Ethiopia. The League of Nations tried sanctions against Ethiopia but not enough countries cooperated.

9. The United States signed a number of neutrality acts in the 1930s. Why didn't the U.S. want to take a stand during the violence of the 1930s? The United States wanted to stay out of foreign problems and wars.

10. a) What aggressive action did Japan commit in 1931? Japan invaded Manchuria.
b) How did the League of Nations respond? The League of Nations condemned the invasion.
c) How did Japan respond? Japan attacked China in 1937.

Appeasement as a Policy

Below are six different questions that will lead you to reasons why Great Britain and France followed a policy of appeasement towards Hitler and Mussolini. They will also help you learn why the United States and the League of Nations did nothing to challenge Japan's aggression against China.

1. How many British and French soldiers and civilians died or were wounded because of World War I? Approximately 5.8 million

2. Some years after the end of World War I, many British and French felt the peace treaties that ended the war were unfair towards Germany. Describe here how the peace treaties treated Germany harshly, and perhaps unfairly. Germany lost land to the victors, could not keep an army, and had to admit war guilt and pay the victors money. Germany was not really the only country at fault.

3. What in America's early history has led the United States to have a strong tradition of isolationism? (Hint: farewell address of George Washington) President George Washington warned Americans not to become involved in foreign wars.

4. From the Russian Revolution of 1917, when the communists seized power, to 1939, the world's democratic governments had a great fear of Soviet communism. The Soviet Communists, under Lenin and then Stalin, had outlawed religion, shut down all churches, killed religious leaders, murdered from 10 – 20 million innocent civilians, and ran the largest work/death camps — the Gulag — known to man. Look at a map. Why would Great Britain and France not mind a stronger Germany? Germany could serve as a buffer between the Soviet Union and Great Britain and France.

5. a) What was the Great Depression? From about 1929 on, the world was in a serious economic crisis. Many were out of work and many were hungry or starving.
b) How did the Great Depression affect the British, the French, and the Americans psychologically? (Did they feel very strong, or weak, because of their difficulties?) The British, French, and Americans felt weak and beaten.

6. Pacifism: a) What is pacifism? Pacifism is the philosophy that is against violence.
b) In which countries were there many pacifists? The United States of America, France, and the United Kingdom

Socratic Discussion and Reflection

When you share ideas with other students, your ideas may be reinforced, rejected, or slightly changed. Listening to your classmates' ideas will help you form your own judgment. After the class discussion, write your reflection.

_____

_____

_____

_____

_____

_____

_____

_____

_____

_____

_____

_____

_____

_____

Week Twenty-Eight: World War II
Socratic Discussion Open-Ended Question
Winning World War II

Why did the Allies win World War II?

Socratic Discussion Open-Ended Question
Dropping the Atomic Bomb

Was the United States correct in dropping the atomic bomb on Japan?

Socratic Discussion Open-Ended Question

Why didn't the United States and the Allies do more to stop the Holocaust?

Socratic Discussion and Reflection

When you share ideas with other students, your ideas may be reinforced, rejected, or slightly changed. Listening to your classmates' ideas will help you form your own judgment. After the class discussion, write your reflection.

_____

_____

_____

_____

_____

_____

_____

_____

_____

_____

_____

_____

_____

_____

Week Twenty-Nine: The Cold War in Europe
Socratic Discussion Open-Ended Question
Fault for the Cold War

Who was at fault for the Cold War?

Socratic Discussion Open-Ended Question
The Cold War in Europe, 1945–1960

According to President Woodrow Wilson, the United States entered into World War I "to make the world safe for democracy." Approximately 20 years after this first Great War, the world fought an even larger and more horrific war. The U.S. goals of World War I were not completely achieved in the first conflict.

In World War II, the America perhaps had simpler goals: stop both Japan and Germany from expanding. In these two aspects, Americans achieved success. The Allies destroyed the militaristic regimes of Japan and Germany and erected new democratic societies in both of these lands. However, the peace of World War II did not bring U.S. troops home. The world still was not safe for democracy, and U.S. troops took a more active role throughout the world. After World War II, the world was split into two main camps — the Communist nations and the democratic nations. American soldiers stationed in Europe and Asia stayed and fought to counter communism and the Soviet Union. Latin America also became the battleground of ideas of communism and democracy. A new kind of war began for America and the world, the Cold War.

Trace the development of the Cold War from its beginnings through the 1950s, focusing mainly on Europe. What was the nature of the Cold War? What was at stake for the United States in the Cold War? Did one society (the Soviet Union or the United States) represent *good* and one society *bad*? What side did the United States support?

You should be familiar with these terms and people:

Josef Stalin	Harry Truman	Potsdam Conference
Marshall Plan	NATO	Iron Curtain
Warsaw Pact	United Nations	Nikita Kruschev
Berlin Airlift	East Berlin (1953)	communism
Poland (1953)	Hungary (1956)	A. Solzhenitsyn
racial segregation	gulag	George Kennan

Compare and Contrast

To compare means to look at two or more objects and recognize what they have in common. To contrast means to look at two or more objects and recognize what they have different from each other.

The United States and the Soviet Bloc, 1945–1960

1. In the United States, how did somebody become the president? How many presidents did the U.S. have between 1945 and 1960? <u>Presidents were elected by the people. From 1945-1960 there were two Presidents.</u>

2. In the Soviet Union, how did somebody become the general secretary of the Communist party (this means, leader of the country)? How many general secretaries did the Soviet Union have between 1945 and 1960? <u>A person used his power to influence powerful people. From 1945 to 1960 there were three leaders of the U.S.S.R.</u>

3. In the United States, what kinds of freedom did a person have regarding his job? Could he choose his own profession? Could he start a business if he wanted to? <u>An American was allowed to choose his own profession and he could start a business if he wanted to.</u>

4. In the Soviet Union and Eastern Europe, what kinds of freedom did a person have regarding his job? Could he choose his own profession? Could he start a business if he wanted to? <u>In Communist Soviet Union and Eastern Europe from 1945-1960, a person did not have complete freedom to choose his own job and could not start a business.</u>

5. Were free speech and free thought protected in the United States? Could an American speak or write freely, or might he be jailed for speaking against the government? <u>Yes</u>

6. Were free speech and free thought protected in the Soviet Union and Eastern Europe? Could a Soviet speak or write freely, or might he be jailed for speaking against the government? <u>A Soviet or Eastern European could be jailed, put in work camps, or killed for speaking against the government.</u>

7. Did Americans have the freedom to practice their own religion? <u>Yes</u>

8. Did Soviets and Eastern Europeans have the freedom to practice their own religion? <u>No. Many churches and synagogues were closed, changed into museums, or destroyed,</u>

9. In the United States or in the Soviet Union were there prisons for political prisoners? How many people are believed to have been prisoners there? <u>The United States did not have political prisons. The U.S.S.R. had the Gulag, a prison system for political prisoners, as well as criminals. It has been impossible to put a number for the political prisoners in the Gulag, but it is certainly over the number believed to have been murdered by the Soviet government from 1917-1989, which numbers from 20-60 million.</u>

10. In the Soviet Union and Eastern Europe, what could have been said to be the greatest injustice in society? _____

_____

11. In the United States, what could have been the greatest injustice in society? _____

_____

_____

The Cold War in Europe, 1945–1960

1. Who were the *Big Three* at the Yalta Conference? <u>Winston Churchill, Franklin Delano Roosevelt, Josef Stalin</u>

2. Who were the *Big Three* at the Potsdam Conference? <u>Clement Atlee, Harry Truman, Josef Stalin</u>

3. What was decided for Germany at these two conferences? <u>The three great powers decided that once defeated, Germany would be split into sections controlled by the victors, and that democratic elections would take place.</u>

4. Concerning democratic elections, what did the Big Three decide for Europe after the war? <u>The Big Three decided that all of Europe would have democratic elections.</u>

5. After World War II, where in Europe were governments democratically elected? Where did democratic elections not take place? <u>Governments were democratically elected in France, Western Germany, Belgium, Luxembourg, Denmark, Sweden, Norway, Finland, Austria, and Italy. Democratic governments were not elected in Soviet controlled Lithuania, Estonia, Latvia, Poland, Czechoslovakia, Hungary, Yugoslavia, and Romania.</u>

6. Where in Europe were there uprisings in 1953 and 1956 that were put down by soldiers? <u>1953: Soviet soldiers crushed an uprising by Eastern Germans. 1956: Soviet soldiers crushed an uprising by Hungary.</u>

7. Why was the Berlin Wall created? <u>The Soviet Union created the Berlin Wall to keep the East Germans from escaping to Western Berlin.</u>

8. What happened to Estonia, Latvia, and Lithuania after World War II? <u>The Soviet Union conquered these lands and its government acted as if all the people in these lands were Russians.</u>

9. What does *satellite country* mean? Did any European country become a satellite of the Soviet Union? <u>When a strong country completely controls a weaker neighbor, the weaker country is known as a satellite.</u>

10. What did Winston Churchill mean when he said that an iron curtain had descended on Europe? <u>Churchill meant that in Eastern Europe, the Soviet Union controlled and oppressed everybody. Freedom was greatly limited in Eastern Europe and in the Soviet Union.</u>

11. Did any European country become a satellite of the United States? <u>One could make the argument that many Latin American governments became satellites of the United States, because of the United States' military and political activities there.</u>

12. What was the Truman doctrine? Was it ever used from 1945–1960? <u>The Truman Doctrine stated that the United States would support free peoples who resisted being taken over.</u>

13. Define the term *Cold War*? <u>The Cold War was when the United States fought the U.S.S.R. through proxies. The system of capitalism was against communism.</u>

14. What year (it's after 1960) did the Cold War end, and how did it end? <u>The Cold War ended in 1989 and 1991. In 1989, the Berlin Wall fell, and communist Eastern Europe gained freedom. In 1991, the Soviet Union fell and splintered into many republics.</u>

Socratic Discussion and Reflection

When you share ideas with other students, your ideas may be reinforced, rejected, or slightly changed. Listening to your classmates' ideas will help you form your own judgment. After the class discussion, write your reflection.

_____

_____

_____

_____

_____

_____

_____

_____

_____

_____

_____

_____

_____

_____

_____

Week Thirty: The End of the Cold War
The Cold War in Asia, Africa, and Latin America, 1945–1980
Socratic Discussion Open-Ended Question

According to President Woodrow Wilson, the United States entered into World War I "to make the world safe for democracy." Approximately 20 years after this first Great War, the world fought an even larger and more horrific war. The U.S. goals of World War I were not completely achieved in the first conflict.

In World War II, the United States perhaps had simpler goals: stop both Japan and Germany from expanding. In these two aspects, Americans achieved success. The Allies destroyed the militaristic regimes of Japan and Germany and erected new democratic societies in both of these lands. However, the peace of World War II did not bring U.S. troops home. The world still was not safe for democracy, and U.S. troops took a more active role throughout the world. After World War II, the world was split into two main camps — the Communist nations and the democratic nations. American soldiers stationed in Europe and Asia stayed and fought to counter communism and the Soviet Union. Latin America also became the battleground of ideas of communism and democracy. A new kind of war began for America and the world, the Cold War.

Trace the development of the Cold War from its beginnings up to 1980, focusing mainly on Asia. What was the nature of the Cold War? What was at stake for the United States in the Cold War? Did one society (the Communist or the democratic) represent *good*, and one society *bad*? What side did the United States support?

To write this essay, you should be familiar with these terms and people:

Mao Tse-Tung	communism	Harry Truman	cultural revolution
Truman doctrine	Potsdam Conference	SEATO	the Vietnamese War
United Nations	Cuban Missile Crisis	Guatemala	Angola
the Congo Republic	the Korean War	Egypt and the Suez Canal (1956)	
Organization of American States (OAS)			

Compare and Contrast
The United States, Democracy, and the Communist World, 1945–1980

1. In the United States, how did somebody become the president? How many presidents did the U.S. have between 1945 and 1980? <u>Presidents were elected. Eight presidents.</u>

2. In China, the leader used to be called the Chairman of the Communist party. How many Chairmen did China have between 1945 and 1980? <u>2</u>

3. In the United States, what kinds of freedom did a person have? Could he choose his own profession? Could he start a business if he wanted to? <u>An American was allowed to choose his own profession and he could start a business if he wanted to.</u>

4. In China and Communist countries of Asia and Latin America, what kinds of freedom did a person have, regarding his job? Could he choose his own profession? Could he start a business if he wanted to? <u>In these countries, a person did not have complete freedom to choose his own job and could not start a business.</u>

5. Were free speech and free thought protected in the United States? Could an American speak or write freely, or might he be jailed for speaking against the government? <u>Yes</u>

6. Were free speech and free thought protected in Communist Asia and Africa? <u>No</u>

7. From 1945 to 1980, how many people were put to death by their own Communist governments? During the same time, how many of its own citizens did the United States and pro–American governments put to death? <u>From 1945-1980, Communist governments killed somewhere between 25-50 million of their own people. From 1945-1980, American and pro-American governments killed somewhere between 500,000 to 1 million people.</u>

8. Did Communist Asians, Africans, and Latin Americans have the freedom to practice their own religion? <u>No.</u>

9. In the United States or in Communist Asia, were there prisons for political prisoners? Where in the world were there death squads? (Death squads were secret police that killed political enemies.) <u>The United States did not have political prisoners, but countries in Communist Asia did. Between 1945-1980, there were death squads in various Latin American countries that were anti-Communist, and death squads were in various Communist Asian countries.</u>

10. Which society fostered greater injustices, the Communist or the democratic? In your answer, provide facts that support your ideas. _____

_____

_____

_____

_____

_____

The Cold War in Asia, Latin America, and Africa, 1945–1980

1. Define the term *Cold War*? The Cold War was when the United States fought the U.S.S.R. through proxies. The U.S. and the U.S.S.R. attempted to win over more of the world to their side of political and economic structures.

2. What was the Truman doctrine? Was it ever used from 1945 to 1980? The Truman Doctrine stated that the United States would help free people defend themselves from outside dominance. In 1947, Greece and Turkey received aid to keep out the communists. The U.S. aided Western Europe and formed NATO to fight against the spread of communism. The U.S. fought in Vietnam and Korea against communists.

3. Describe the U.S. policy of *containment* towards communism. American George F. Kennan argued that the Soviet Union would destroy itself if it was not allowed to expand.

4. In the Middle East, of which country in the late 1940s was the United States an ally? Israel

5. Which country did the Soviet Union support in the Middle East in the 1950s? Egypt, Iran, and Iraq

6. Who set up a pro-Communist government in Iraq in July 1958? Brigadier General Adbul Karim Qassim

7. In the Republic of the Congo, which type of government was formed after independence was won from France in 1960? A Republic was formed, but in 1969 this country became communist and was renamed The People's Republic of the Congo.

8. In Angola in 1975, Angola won its independence from Portugal. Describe the situation that followed in Angola. Various factions fought each other until the late 1990s. In the 1970s and 1980s the U.S., the U.S.S.R., and Cuba sent money and military aid to democratic or communist factions.

9. Why did many Cubans support Fidel Castro in the Cuban revolution of 1959? What type of government did he set up? Cubans supported Fidel Castro because the Cuban leader Batista ran a government that was corrupt and a police force that treated Cubans poorly. Cubans were also poor and the future looked grim.

10. Very briefly describe the Cuban Missile Crisis. In October 1962, the United States challenged the Soviet Union's building nuclear missile sites on Cuba. After a U.S. naval quarantine around Cuba, the Soviet Union dismantled the nuclear missiles, the U.S. promised to never invade Cuba and it dismantled its nuclear missiles in Turkey.

11. Describe a brief political history of Chile, from 1970 to 1980. Prime Minister Salvador Allende (1970-73) attempted socialist changes in Chile, nationalizing key industries and instituting agrarian reforms. The military took over in 1973 under Augusto Pinochet. The anti-communist leader oversaw human rights violations and economic gains.

12. Describe what happened in Guatemala from 1950 to 1980. The U.S. sponsored anti-communist and anti-democratic governments who fought with communists, killing hundreds of thousands of Guatemalans.

13. What was the Korean War? Communist North Koreans, Chinese, and Russians fought democratic South Korea and free countries from the League of Nations led by the United States. The war lasted from 1950-1953, leaving Korea split into communist North Korea and democratic South Korea. Approximately 54,000 U.S. soldiers died in the Korean War.

14. What was the Vietnam War? <u>Communist North Vietnam, China, and the Soviet Union fought the United States, South Vietnam, and South Korea from 1965-1973. After the U.S withdrew in 1973 and failed to provide financial support for South Vietnam, North Vietnam conquered the South in 1975. Approximately 58,000 U.S. soldiers died in the Vietnam War.</u>

Socratic Discussion Open-Ended Question
The Korean and the Vietnam War

Was the United States justified in fighting the Korean War and the Vietnam War?

Socratic Discussion Open-Ended Question
The Warsaw Pact and NATO

Compare and contrast the Warsaw Pact with NATO. Which organization was established purely for defensive reasons? Did one side represent good, and one represent evil? In which was there more liberty? In which were there political prisoners?

Socratic Discussion Open-Ended Question
The End of the Cold War

What role did President Reagan and Pope John Paul II play in toppling the Communist governments of Europe?

Socratic Discussion and Reflection

When you share ideas with other students, your ideas may be reinforced, rejected, or slightly changed. Listening to your classmates' ideas will help you form your own judgment. After the class discussion, write your reflection.

_____

_____

_____

_____

_____

_____

_____

_____

_____

_____

_____

_____

_____

_____

_____

_____

Week Thirty-One
The Post-Cold War World and Islamic Terrorism

Socratic Discussion Open-Ended Question
Should France Ban Women From Wearing Head Scarves?

Socratic Discussion Open-Ended Question
Why did the 9/11 Terrorists Attack the U.S.A.?

Socratic Discussion Open-Ended Question
Should the U.S.A. have Waged War Against Iraq?

Socratic Discussion Open-Ended Question
Should President Obama Responded to Assad Atrocities Stronger?

Socratic Discussion Open-Ended Question
How did ISIS Expand its Territory?

Socratic Discussion Open-Ended Question
What is the Best Way for the U.S. to Fight Islamic Terrorism?

Socratic Discussion Open-Ended Question
What is the main reason for world Anti-Semitism and Anti-Christian Persecution?

Socratic Discussion Open-Ended Question
According to Jacques Ellul, what are the core ideals of the Western Tradition? Are these ideals good for all people?

Week Thirty Two
Final Class
Which topic was your favorite to study, learn, and talk about this year?